GOD GRANT

GOD GRANT

365 Christ-Centered
Daily Meditations for Recovery

PAUL F. KELLER

HarperSanFrancisco
A Division of HarperCollins*Publishers*

GOD GRANT: *365 Christ-Centered Daily Meditations for Recovery.* Copyright © 1989 by Paul F. Keller. All rights reserved. Printed in the United States of America. No part of this book may be used or reproduced in any manner whatsoever without written permission except in the case of brief quotations embodied in critical articles and reviews. For information address HarperCollins Publishers, 10 East 53rd Street, New York, NY 10022.

Library of Congress Cataloging-in Publication Data

Keller, Paul F., 1922–
    God grant : 365 Christ-centered daily meditations
for recovery / Paul F. Keller. — 1st ed.
        p.   cm.
    ISBN 0-6-64304-8 : $8.95
    1. Alcoholics—Prayer-books and devotions—English.
2. Devotional calendars.   I. Title.
BV4596.A48K45   1989
242′.4—dc20
                                        89-45186
                                        CIP

    91 92 93 KP 10 9 8 7 6 5 4 3

INTRODUCTION

This book is for people who have admitted they were powerless over alcohol or other drugs; people whose lives had become unmanageable.

It is for people who have come to believe that only a Power greater than themselves can restore them to sanity; people who have made a decision to turn their will and lives over to the care and keeping of God.

Such people may be finding their strength and hope in one of many fellowships dedicated to sobriety, spiritual growth, and sane lifestyles.

Based on the four Gospels and Twelves Steps for recovery, our hope and prayer is for ever-deepening commitment to Christ—a longer and lasting growth into abundant love, hope, and joy.

This book is meant for people who want more of God's love, Christ's fellowship, and the Holy Spirit's power.

HOW TO USE THIS BOOK

Each daily meditation is based on a verse from one of the four Gospels in the New Testament. If you have a Bible with you, you may want to read the entire passage in which the verse for the day appears. Seeing the verse in its context will help you understand it better.

These daily meditations can be used in several ways.

You may read one silently by yourself. Read slowly, pausing after each sentence or paragraph to meditate on what is being said. Reflect on your own life—where you have come from, where you are now, where you are going. Apply the message to your own life. Let the words sink deeply into you.

Take time to answer the questions that follow the reading.

Pause before you read the prayer. You may want to picture Jesus standing before you and imagine yourself speaking the prayer directly to him. You can add your own words of prayer, bringing your deepest needs and hopes to God.

The closing statement is a summary thought to carry with you. If you read the meditation in the morning, you could memorize the statement or write it on a piece of paper and carry it with you in your purse or wallet. In this way you can reflect on it often during the day. You might also wish to carry the Bible verse or prayer with you. If you read the meditation at the end of the day, you can reflect on the summary statement as you fall asleep.

A second way to use these meditations, if conditions permit, is to read them aloud to yourself in God's presence. When you speak the words and hear them, they enter more deeply into your mind and heart. Again, pause between sections to apply the thoughts to your personal experience.

You could also use these meditations in a group setting. You might first read aloud the entire Bible passage in which the key verse is embedded, then repeat the key verse. As you continue to read the meditation, be sure to leave moments of silence during which group members can do their personal reflection. After the prayer, some members may want to add their own brief sentence prayers. Close by reading aloud the summary thought.

As you meditate on God's Word as we find it in the Gospels, God grant that you grow in relationship to Christ, in freedom from addiction, in faith and love, in hope and joy.

GOD GRANT

Finding Rest for Our Souls

"Come unto me, all you who are weary and burdened, and I will give you rest."—MATTHEW 11:28

We know what it is to be powerless, for our lives to be unmanageable.

We know what it is to feel sick and tired, worn down, hopeless, and helpless.

We know the weight of heavy burdens, the guilt, shame, remorse, fear, anger, resentment, and hopelessness.

We know what it is to do violence to ourselves, to others, and to God.

We know what it is to seek rest for our souls, because that's what our addictions were meant to provide: Rest for our souls.

Christ offers us rest for our souls as we work our program for recovery, one day at a time.

Have I admitted that I am powerless over my addictions? Am I responding positively to Christ's invitation to find rest for my soul?

God grant that I may find rest for my soul.

There is a place of quiet rest; near to the heart of God.

January 2

COMING TO BELIEVE

> *"I do believe; help me overcome my unbelief!"*—MARK 9:24

We need help. We pray for deliverance from doubt and confusion. We pray to be restored to sanity.

We come to believe that God can do for us what we cannot do for ourselves: that God can restore us to sanity.

We let go of doubt and unbelief.

We trust God with our lives, seeking only to know God's will and to have the power to carry it out.

We are on our road to recovery, to new life, new hope, and new joy.

Christ leads us into sanity as we work our program for recovery one day at a time.

Am I believing that I can be restored to sanity? Am I trusting God with my life and recovery?

God grant that I may be restored to sanity.

Believing God is being restored to sanity.

MAKING A DECISION

> *"For whoever wants to save his life will lose it, but whoever loses his life for me will save it . . ."*—LUKE 9:24

Many of us were threatened with the loss of family, friends, jobs, financial security, and self-respect.

And some of us lost everything.

Filled with selfishness and self-centeredness we had nothing left but our stubborn willfulness.

The bottom we hit was alarmingly painful.

We began to see that we would have to change and be changed.

We made a decision to turn our will and our lives over to the care and keeping of God.

At that moment things began to change, and we started to heal.

As we work our program for recovery, Christ is able to change us, one day at a time.

Am I believing God? Am I turning my will and life over to the care and keeping of the Lord?

God grant that I may make a decision to be changed.

Making a decision to change is when everything begins for the better.

January 4

TAKING ANOTHER LOOK AT OURSELVES

"Repent, for the kingdom of heaven is near."—MATTHEW 3:2

How many times have we wished that life could be different for us? Better. Quietly serene. Beautiful.

And, we thought, life could be that way if only people would change. If only the world would change.

Then, by the grace of God, we came to sense—if at first very dimly—that other people are not our problem, nor is the world.

We began to make a searching and fearless moral inventory of ourselves.

We made a list of our character defects, beginning with dishonesty: dishonesty with ourselves, dishonesty with others, and dishonesty with God.

Afraid as we were to look carefully at ourselves, we were making a decision to recover, to heal.

Christ provides the courage we need to be honest with ourselves, one day at a time.

Am I taking searching and fearless moral inventories of myself? Am I being honest with myself, with others, with God?

God grant that I may be fearlessly honest.

Being honest is a lot easier than being dishonest.

DOING SOMETHING HELPFUL FOR OURSELVES

Confessing their sins, they were baptized by him in the Jordan river.—MATTHEW 3:6

We become ready to take responsibility for what we have done with our lives, for sins committed against ourselves, against others, against God.

We confess our sins—the exact nature of our wrongs—to ourselves, to another human being (priest, pastor, counselor, friend), and to God. By so doing, we experience release from burdens that have become too heavy for us to bear.

Not only has God forgiven us, but we have also released ourselves from feelings of guilt and shame.

We are baptized in the healing power of God, given strength and courage to go on with trust and confidence in Christ. One day at a time.

Am I ready to confess my sins, to come clean with my life? Am I ready to be immersed in the power of God in order to heal?

God grant me the courage to confess my sins, to be healed.

Sincere confession releases us to celebrate new life, new hope, and new joy.

January 6

BECOMING ENTIRELY READY

> *"Produce fruit in keeping with repentance."*—MAT-
> THEW 3:8

We admitted that we are powerless, believing that only God could restore us to sanity.

We began to turn our wills and our lives over to God.

We made a fearless and searching moral inventory of our lives.

We confessed our sins to ourselves, to God, and to another human being.

The next step is as big as any: We become entirely ready to have God remove all defects of character: fear, anger, resentment, lust, and dishonesty.

We become ready for God to work the miracle of healing in our lives, bringing us into recovery.

When we are powerless, Christ is able to help us—one day at a time.

Am I entirely ready to have God change me? Am I entirely willing to have God remove all of my character defects?

God grant me the courage to change and be changed.

Becoming ready for God to work miracles in us is more than half the battle.

HUMBLY ASKING

"And do not think you can say to yourself 'we have Abraham as our father.' "—MATTHEW 3:9

Recovery is not about making excuses for ourselves or anyone else. Nor is it meant that we should crawl under the weight of guilt and shame.

Recovery is about accepting personal responsibility for ourselves and our lives, including the wrongs we have done.

We make no excuses for ourselves, what we have done with our lives and left undone.

We humbly ask God to remove all of our shortcomings, our defects of character, our sins.

We do not ask for the removal of defects in others. We only humbly ask for shortcomings to be removed from ourselves.

Am I humbly asking God to remove my shortcomings? Am I sincere about my desire to be renewed in the Spirit of God?

God grant me the courage to take responsibility for my own life and behavior.

Humbly asking is not crawling. Crawling is not being humble.

BECOMING WILLING

> *"He will baptize you with the Holy Spirit and fire."*
> —MATTHEW 3:11

The Gospel leaves us with tremendous promises, such as the one we have in our scripture for today.

We are promised that new power is going to be given, new Spirit and new fire, something beyond ourselves: something we cannot dig up on our own.

This power comes from God and fills us with strength we never knew possible—strength to make a list of everyone we have harmed, becoming willing to make amends to them all.

We are not asked to do everything at once, only that we be willing to do what God enables us to do right now.

Am I ready to receive God's power? Am I willing to make amends to those I have harmed?

God grant me readiness and willingness to receive the Holy Spirit's power into my life.

Sometimes making a list is the only workable way to begin very important and life-saving projects.

MAKING AMENDS

> *"Every tree that does not produce good fruit will be cut down and thrown into the fire."*—MATTHEW 3:10

We make direct amends to people we have harmed, wherever possible, "except when to do so would injure them or others."

We settle accounts where they can be settled, paying unpaid debts.

We realize that being ready to rectify, to make right and to restore, is never easy.

But once it is over, once we have done our best to make restitution, we have done what is necessary to strengthen our recovery. And that is sufficient.

By so doing we begin to experience tranquility, serenity, peace.

Am I making direct amends to people I have wronged? Am I setting myself free from needless guilt and shame?

God grant me the power to make amends.

Honestly settling accounts is the doorway to a new life of freedom.

BELIEVING THAT SOMEONE IS BIGGER

> *"But after me will come one who is more powerful than I."*—MATTHEW 3:11

The recognition that someone or something is greater than we are is basic to a lasting recovery.

No longer are we King Tut, the Queen of Sheba, or God.

God is God. Christ is the Lord. We are children of God, and God is greater than we are.

Believing in a power greater than ourselves is essential to recovery and ongoing healthy sobriety.

But false pride always rears its ugly head, trying again and again to get us to what we imagine is the head of the line.

Recovery is coming to realize and affirm that God is more powerful than we are; that God, in Christ, has the power to save us from self-destruction.

Am I willing to believe that God is more powerful than I am? Am I willing to turn my will and my life over to the care and keeping of Christ?

God grant me the gifts of humility, acceptance, and surrender.

Surrendering to real power is a very great step forward.

BEING PURIFIED

> *"His winnowing fork is in his hand, and he will clear his threshing floor, gathering the wheat into the barn."*
> —MATTHEW 3:12

Once we are seriously set on recovery into sobriety we can count on everything coming out on the threshing floor—both the good grain and the chaff.

Make no mistake about it: Recovery is not for anyone who doesn't want to be winnowed, to be threshed out.

And we may go down screaming before we are gathered in and given new life.

It's not easy to stop being a liar and cheat. But that's what we have to do: stop lying to ourselves, to others, and to God; stop cheating ourselves of the new life of healthy sobriety.

Most certainly there is pain involved in recovery, but this doesn't mean it's bad pain, as we once thought and feared.

What is useless for our recovery must go. What is clear and comforting will stay.

Am I willing to be cleansed of my deceptiveness? Am I ready to have God do it?

God grant me the willingness to be cleansed of all deceptiveness.

God's first intention is to purify us.

January 12

BEING BURNED CLEAN

> " . . . burning up the chaff with unquenchable fire.'
> —MATTHEW 3:12

How far does this cleansing process have to go?
How much of ourselves do we have to give up?

We have to give up everything that gets in the
way of our recovery into spiritual growth and development.

If we actually want to stay sober, the chaff of
self-will must go.

Everything that hinders our salvation must be
burned, as with fire: the chaff of stiffened egos, the
chaff of self-will running riot, the chaff of fear, anger,
and resentment.

Praying to the Lord to cleanse us in the fires of
repentance and renewal is a basic part of our recovery into new life, new hope, and new joy.

We don't necessarily like the heat of purgation,
but we come to welcome the cleansing. Believe it or
not.

Am I willing to be cleansed by the power of God?
Am I willing to come clean with my life?

*God grant me the courage to be purified by the fire
of your love.*

Cleansing hurts, but leaves us feeling much better

BEING LED THROUGH

Then Jesus was led by the Spirit into the desert to be tempted by the devil.—MATTHEW 4:1

The one who saves us from ourselves is Jesus, who was tempted as we are tempted; who entered into our temptations in order to be part of us, to show us the love of God for the creation and each one of us.

Always there will be temptation to sin, to fall short, to become separated from God, and we don't have to feel guilty about being tempted.

Nor do we have to worry about being swallowed up by temptations to use again, because the Lord is with us.

In the great temptation Jesus stood firm, not by himself alone, but in the power of God. And that same power of God is made available through Christ, who strengthens us.

Our Lord has shown us that it is possible to live through temptations, by turning ourselves completely over to God's care and keeping.

Am I aware of temptations to use again? Am I trusting Jesus to lead me through?

God grant me victory over all temptations to break my sobriety.

Deliver us from evil, for thine is the power.

January 14

TRUSTING THE HEALING POWER

> *People brought to him all who were ill with various diseases, those suffering severe pain, the demon-possessed, the epileptics, and the paralytic, and he healed them.*—MATTHEW 4:24

What better way is there to describe the nature of our lives before we turned our wills and our lives over to the care and keeping of God?

Were we not diseased, suffering pain, demon-possessed, having seizures?

Is not this an accurate description of how we were?

Were we not at times mentally and spiritually paralyzed?

Then, one miraculous day, it happened! We were stopped in our tracks—brought into the presence of God's healing power and turned around.

On that day of miracles our lives began to be restored, made new, reborn.

Am I making myself available? Am I entrusting myself to the healing power of Christ?

God grant me the readiness to be healed.

Turning to Jesus for healing, day by day, is real and lasting sobriety.

BEING SPIRITUALLY RECEPTIVE

> *"Blessed are the poor in spirit, for theirs is the kingdom of heaven."*—MATTHEW 5:3

Being poor in spirit is being receptive to all that God is ready to supply for our recovery.

Being poor in spirit is knowing and believing that our salvation comes from God as a gift, and that the gift cannot be earned.

Being poor in spirit is humbly offering ourselves, each and every day, to God's care and keeping.

Being poor in spirit is seeking to do God's will.

Knowing that we are spiritually poor, that we are blind, deaf, and dumb in spiritual matters, is of utmost importance if we want a good and lasting recovery.

Rising up from near spiritual death is what recovery is all about.

Am I receptive to God's healing gifts? Am I ready to accept what God offers to bring about my recovery?

God grant me spiritual growth into newness of life.

Being poor in spirit is being alive in God.

January 16

FEELING SAD

> *"Blessed are those who mourn, for they will be comforted."*—MATTHEW 5:4

Separation and sorrow, grief and mourning, are all part of our recovery. We deeply miss our old "friends"—the bottle, the pills, the substances—that once made us feel so right, so good, so comfortable.

With sobriety there is the sense of loss. And with suffered loss there is always sorrow, even mourning.

However, comfort begins to come when we give ourselves permission to be sad, to mourn, to weep and lament for a time. After all, we have lost what seemed to be a very good friend: our bottle, the substances, the tranquilizers that once made us feel so comfortable, so on top of it, so sure of ourselves.

Eventually the sad feelings give way to gladness, as we consciously experience the healing comfort of God's grace.

Am I aware of my loss? Am I aware of my grief?

God grant me comfort in days of sadness.

Being sad is not being bad.

BEING MEEK TO INHERIT

"Blessed are the meek, for they will inherit the earth."
—MATTHEW 5:5

Grandiosity can be one of the by-products of our addiction: taking credit for staying sober, playing God, knowing everything and more.

Grandiosity is also not seeking help, pretending to be self-sufficient, staying away from meetings, not reading our books, not working our program.

We are grandiose when we pretend to know what we don't know, pretend to be self-sufficient, get the big head, say "See what I have done! Look at me!"

To be meek is the opposite of all this. It is to be humbly patient, trusting God to lead, to guide, to uphold, to help, to save. And to be humbly patient is to be sober indeed.

Am I being humbly patient in my sobriety, trusting God to give me new life, new hope, and new joy? Day by day, am I giving God credit for my sobriety?

God grant me the freedom to be who I really am, without frills.

To be meek is to be humbly patient, is to be sober.

HUNGERING AND THIRSTING

> *"Blessed are those who hunger and thirst for righteousness, for they will be filled."*—MATTHEW 5:6

Righteousness?

We insisted on righteousness, demanded that others be upright and moral, spotlessly clean.

We didn't know much about true righteousness, but we knew a great deal about being self-righteous.

With God's help we are becoming more able to drop our self-righteousness and more eager for God to rule our lives; more able to seek gratification by serving God and others—by carrying the message of recovery to those who still suffer—by being honest and truthful in all of our affairs—by hungering and thirsting for the righteousness of God.

With Christ as our Master we come to consciously desire God, to do what God wants of us, to stand upright, to be virtuous.

Am I hungering and thirsting for God? Am I seeking true righteousness and virtue in Christ?

God grant me the gifts of true righteousness and virtue in Christ.

Hungering and thirsting for true righteousness is the way of sobriety.

BEING MERCIFUL

> *"Blessed are the merciful, for they will be shown mercy."*—MATTHEW 5:7

Mercy? We expected a lot of mercy.

We expected God and others to be merciful to us, when we were drunk and hung over; when we treated others badly and behaved obnoxiously.

People were supposed to understand our predicament.

But now there is a new and different life-giving ingredient in our lives.

Now we know, for certain, that without God's merciful acceptance of us—just as we are—we are lost, beyond recovery and beyond hope.

It is healing to learn of God's mercy, but even more so to receive it with thanksgiving.

It is healing and life-giving to show mercy to others as God is merciful to us.

Am I receiving God's mercy into my life? Am I being merciful as God is merciful to me?

God grant me a heart filled with mercy.

"The quality of mercy is not strained,
It droppeth as the gentle rain from heaven."
—William Shakespeare, *The Merchant of Venice*

January 20

BEING PURIFIED BY LOVE

"Blessed are the pure in heart, for they will see God."
—MATTHEW 5:8

If there was one thing we wanted to believe about ourselves, it was that we were honest and pure of heart, with good motives, always trying to be helpful.

What an illusion that was.

And how long does it take to see through the darkness of self-deception, to see what really has happened, to see the true condition of our hearts and spirits before we stopped using?

No wonder we could find no real peace, contentment, serenity, happiness—not with all of the lying and cheating and fooling of ourselves.

Now, however, with the program of recovery and the power of God in Christ our Lord, things are beginning to be changed for the better, slowly but surely.

Now we are beginning to see more of God at work in our own lives and the lives of others—because our hearts are being purified by love.

Am I being honest with myself, with others, with God? Am I being purified day by day?

God grant me the gift of a pure heart.

God i. seen through a pure heart.

BEING PEACEMAKERS

> *"Blessed are the peacemakers, for they will be called sons of God."*—MATTHEW 5:9

Today's scripture applies to all recovering people, inasmuch as peacemaking is the major event in sobriety—finding peace with ourselves, with others, and with God.

This doesn't mean that we try to make others over, try to bend people into being peacemakers.

It means that we see our work to be that of delivering the gift of peace in this strife-torn world, which we are empowered to do.

We are able to be peacemakers because we are stepping outside of our little inverted domain, away from self-will running riot.

We are enabled to make peace, to right the wrongs we have done, to make amends to those we have harmed, to bless the world with our new-found presence.

All of this because we are sons and daughters of God.

Am I being a peacemaker? Am I living at peace with myself, with others, and with God?

God grant me the grace to be a peacemaker.

Peacemakers are what God intends us to be.

January 22

BEING PATIENT IN RECOVERY

"Blessed are those who are persecuted because of righteousness, for theirs is the kingdom of heaven."—MATTHEW 5:10

We catch on quickly: Recovery is not precisely the way we had envisioned it. There are a lot of rocks in the road.

There may be those who have labeled us derelicts, who can't accept the fact that we are changing.

Because of this we may not only feel misunderstood, but even persecuted.

Even though all of this may be part of the process, recovery is highly rewarding—as long as we keep on with our program, paying strict attention to ourselves and not taking on any kind of ill will that may be coming our way.

It is through patience and surrender that we begin to understand that the Kingdom of heaven also belongs to us, regardless of what others may say or do.

Am I seeing myself as being misunderstood, and persecuted? Am I being patient?

God grant that I may not be overcome by any ill will directed at me.

It's not what other people do to us that counts, but what we do with ourselves.

ACCEPTING WHAT COMES

> *"Blessed are you when people insult you, persecute you, and falsely say all kinds of evil against you because of me."*—MATTHEW 5:11

Being a follower of Christ, in our sobriety, is the most productive way of life that we can have. But there are hazards.

People do not always understand what we are about. In fact, most people don't.

Old drinking "friends" will not want us around, if they are still drinking. This can feel like an insult, as if we're being mistreated.

Granted, this kind of rejection isn't like going to the lions, but it can be painful, causing some to stumble.

It is up to us to be ready for such occurrences and to stay with our program.

We have the assurance that Christ is going to be with us all the way, through thick and thin—giving us the needed strength to carry on and to heal.

Am I maintaining my confidence in God? Am I able to accept whatever anyone thinks or says about me?

God grant that I may stay with my program at all costs.

Christ gives us all the power we need, for all circumstances we must face.

January 24

REMEMBERING WHO AND WHAT WE ARE

> *"You are the salt of the earth."*—MATTHEW 5:13

When we are working our program and staying sober, we are the salt of the earth.

And if we slip—God forbid—we run the risk of losing everything.

Losing our sobriety sets us up to become totally lost to ourselves, to others, and to God. It is something we never want to happen, and that is why we avoid the first drink, which could be our last drink, and the open grave.

For us there can be no such risk as taking a first drink. But should this happen, and if we are able, it is time to get back into the program as soon as possible, before we lose everything.

We must remember that we are people of value, that we have something to offer the world by being who we are, as sober human beings: God's beloved, the salt of the earth.

Am I remembering who I am, as a sober person? Am I remembering that I am important to the earth and to God?

God grant that I am as a child of God, the salt of the earth.

Being what God has created and redeemed us to be is to be the salt of the earth.

BEING A LIGHT TO OTHERS

"You are the light of the world."—MATTHEW 5:14

There's a little song that says, "This little light of mine, I'm going to let it shine . . . let it shine . . . all the time."

Keeping our sobriety is remembering this light and how much others who suffer need the light, how much they need our sobriety to support their own.

This is because staying sober isn't an individual accomplishment. It happens and is best maintained in community where we can see other lights, where individual lights can be brought together to make beautiful light for everyone to see.

As recovering people, we are called to gather others into the program, not by promotion but by attraction, by what we do with our lives; by staying sober and growing in Christ our Lord.

Let us remember that sober we are light in darkness. This is a high calling, in which we can rejoice.

Am I being the light of Christ to others? Am I seeing the importance of my sobriety to others?

God grant that I may be a little flicker of light in darkness.

It is better to be a little flicker than no light at all.

BEING SEEN BY OTHERS

"A city on a hill cannot be hidden."—MATTHEW 5:14

People are not going to notice our sobriety all that much, except for those who are naturally close to us.

The world goes on as usual, whether we are sober or not.

Still, we are not hidden. Anonymous, yes, but not hidden.

We go to our work and play, and are not hidden. Quiet, yes, but not hidden.

We are called to let the light of our sobriety quietly shine among people, so they may see the good that is happening to us and give praise to God.

There is no way to hide a change of character and lifestyle once it really begins to happen.

Through our own sobriety others are brought into newness of life.

Am I aware of God working through me? Do I see myself as an extension of God's love and light to others who suffer?

God grant that I may be used to help others who suffer.

There's no hiding change once it actually begins.

MAKING AMENDS

> *"If you . . . remember that your brother has something against you, leave your gift there in front of the altar. First go and be reconciled to your brother; then come and offer your gift."*—MATTHEW 5:23–24

Because we have not reached perfection, we are bound to encounter conflict.

The chances are good that we will have left an unsavory trail of strained, if not broken, relationships in the wake of our using. So, for the sake of a healthy sobriety, we must make the move to go to the offended brother or sister and make amends.

This means simply to listen to those who have something against us, giving them the opportunity to ventilate, rather than trying to set them straight, rather than denying our offences or making excuses.

Then, we become right with ourselves, with others, and with God—whether our offer to make amends has been accepted or not.

Am I making amends to those I have offended? Am I being honest with myself and others?

God grant that I may rebuild the bridges of my life.

Rebuilding bridges reconnects us to ourselves, others, and God.

January 28

BEING ABSOLUTELY HONEST

> *"You have heard that it was said, 'Do not commit adultery.' But I tell you: anyone who looks at a woman lustfully has already committed adultery with her in his heart."*—MATTHEW 5:27–28

So what's new? We're all human, and "everyone lusts."

But that's not the issue.

Our humanity is not being questioned. We are simply being informed of the way things are.

The great danger to our sobriety is dishonesty: pretending that we are interested in someone else as a person, when we are actually misusing them sexually or any other way.

When we use anyone, for any reason, we are taking dangerous steps toward a slip.

A great danger to our sobriety is *not* to see ourselves as we are, and to treat others dishonestly.

Am I aware of my inner self and motives? Am I being honest with myself, with others, and with God?

God grant that I may be honest in all things.

Lying to ourselves short circuits any hope for a healthy sobriety.

Doing What's Necessary

"If your eye causes you to sin, gouge it out and throw it away."—MATTHEW 5:29

Sobriety includes decision making, and not all decisions are easy. When we stopped using, we made a painful decision to cut off and throw away something near and dear to us, but also deadly.

There still may be times when we are confronted with needs and desires that seem overwhelming: temptations to try it again. Maybe just one drink, one pill, one anything. Just to see if we might get that old mellow feeling back again.

We see something we want to have again, even though it's deadly: "If your eye sees something it wants that is going to kill you, get rid of your eye." That's how important the new life is, with its new hope and new joy. Christ empowers us to get rid of all that would prevent our rebirth.

Am I serious about my sobriety? Am I willing to do whatever is necessary to keep it?

God grant that I may do all that is needed to keep my sobriety.

Sometimes it is very painful to do what has to be done, to save our sobriety and our lives.

January 30

KEEPING IT SIMPLE AND QUIET

> *"Simply let your 'Yes' be 'Yes,' and your 'No,' 'No.' "*
> —MATTHEW 5:37

Jesus is talking about taking vows, making promises, doing a lot of needless talking about what we are going to do next.

We did all of that: swore to stop using, promised never to do it again, and some of us with our hands on the Bible.

Now, all of that nonsensical uselessness can be shortened considerably:

Fewer words.

No promises.

There is a lot to be said for silence.

People who practice silence over a period of time discover that refraining from big talk really helps the recovery process.

What is more, we don't have anything to prove when we are staying sober. Our sobriety will do its own work in that regard.

Simply and quietly.

Am I making any needless vows or promises? Am I keeping things simple and quiet?

God grant that I may keep my life simple and quiet.

It's not what we say but what we do that counts.

REFUSING REVENGE

> *"If someone strikes you on the right cheek, turn to him the other also."*—MATTHEW 5:39

There are some things we must learn to live without—such as resentment and revenge.

We have no room for this kind of energy. Because, for us, it is a certain way to return to a destructive life.

If there are those who have wronged us, we must choose some response other than resentment and revenge.

Jesus understood the futility of resentment and revenge—not only the futility, but the self-destructiveness.

So when he says, "turn the other cheek," Jesus simply means for us to refuse vengeful reactions against those who have wronged us.

The truth is that we don't have to attend every fight to which we are invited.

Am I carrying any grudges? Am I seeking any revenge?

God grant that I carry no grudges and seek no revenge.

Grudges and revenge get us nowhere except drunk and dead.

February 1

REFUSING NEEDLESS CONFLICT

> *"And if someone wants to sue you and take your tunic, let him have your cloak as well."*—MATTHEW 5:40

What is the very best for us in our program for sobriety?

Certainly it isn't compliance, doing something against our will, pretending to be in a state of acceptance and forgiveness when we are still harboring grudges, still filled with resentment and desire for revenge.

"Back off," Jesus says, but with one more step: Offer something more than resistance.

Extend a helping and forgiving hand.

Whether it be accepted or rejected makes no difference, for it's in the extra effort, the extended hand, that we find new life in our sobriety.

The wisdom of Jesus is based on powerful spiritual principles that work together for our good: acceptance, forgiveness, surrender, and dedication to service.

Am I refusing needless conflict? Am I extending myself beyond compliance, resentment, and getting even?

God grant that I may refuse needless conflict.

Needless conflict is not an ingredient for healthy sobriety.

FREELY GIVING AND LIVING

> *"Give to the one who asks you, and do not turn away from the one who wants to borrow from you."*—MATTHEW 5:42

Giving what we have to offer is fundamental to our program for recovery.

Having been blessed with the lifting of our affliction, we must be ready to serve those who need what we have.

For instance, we have our own story to tell, how it was with us, how it is now, and what a difference sobriety is making in our lives.

Our work is to spread the blessings we have received.

Having had a spiritual awakening as the result of these steps we try to carry this message to others who suffer, to practice these principles in all our affairs.

Our joyous opportunity is too give what is asked of us, to share what has been given to us.

This is a very real part of growing spiritually, staying sober, and doing some honest-to-goodness living.

Am I giving what has been given to me? Am I holding anything back?

God grant that I may hold nothing back that has been given to me.

Give. Give. Give. The way to sobriety.

LOVING AND FORGIVING

> *"Love your enemies and pray for those who persecute you."*—MATTHEW 5:44

In our recovery process we are urged to love as we are being loved, to give as it has been given to us.

Carrying resentments and grudges is exceptionally dangerous for people like us.

The moment we even think about retaliation we are in trouble with ourselves, and our sobriety is on slippery ground.

But neither is it enough to hide our feelings, pretending that it makes no difference that someone has done us wrong.

Jesus offers us an opportunity to do something constructive when someone hurts us: pray for those who mistreat us—not that God will strike them dead, but that the Lord will bless all of us with the gift of peace.

Am I willing to let go of resentment? Am I willing to pray for those who mistreat me?

God grant that I may carry no resentments.

There is no one who can harm us more than we can harm ourselves.

Loving the Unlovable

*"If you only love those who love you, what reward will
'ou get?"*—matthew 5:46

Can you think of anything more disgusting than
a falling-down drunk who refuses the help you have
to offer? And even worse, someone who stomps on
you unfairly?

It's easy to love the members of our squad, to love
people who are building us up with encouragement
in our recovery. But what about the seemingly unlovable?

Loving the unlovable isn't easy. And there are
those who will tell us that we were very difficult to
love while we were using, and sometimes difficult to
love even in our sobriety.

However, when we are able to love the unlovable
we are strengthened in our sobriety.

But we need power greater than ourselves to love
the unlovable. And Christ is that power.

Let us pray for the power to love the unlovable.
Then let's make certain we do so.

Am I reaching out to the unlovable? Am I carrying
the message to those who still suffer?

God grant that I love the unlovable.

Loving others as we are loved is the work of recovery.

February 5

BEING CAREFUL AND QUIET

*"Be careful not to do your 'acts of righteousness'
before men, to be seen by them."*—MATTHEW 6:1

There are reasons for not blowing our horns about
our sobriety. And there are good reasons for doing
things for others without anyone knowing about it.

Not showing ourselves off for others, so as to be
seen and glorified, is essential for our sobriety, our
spiritual growth and development.

Healing recovery is strengthened by attraction
rather than promotion.

We do what we have been given to do by the
Lord, without asking to be seen or rewarded. The
reward is in the doing of the deed itself. Quietly. Not
in a spotlight.

This is not always easy for most of us to do, especially with our need to be seen, loved, and adored.

So, when we do something good for someone else,
it is best to keep it as secret as possible.

That way our sobriety will be strengthened as we
grow in the Spirit of our Lord Jesus Christ.

Am I working my program quietly? Am I practicing
my gift of sobriety with quiet gratitude to God?

God grant that I may not do good to be seen by others.

Showing off our good works won't keep us sober.

KEEPING A LOW PROFILE

> *"When you give to the needy, do not announce it with trumpets."*—MATTHEW 6:2

We must always remember the importance of keeping a low profile.

In the traditions of our recovery program, it is essential to do what we can to help those in need. It is equally important to keep ourselves away from center stage.

This happens naturally when we see ourselves as humble servants of Christ, and realize that it is not we who are doing the good work, but Christ working in and through us.

Whatever we do to help, we do it quietly, as humble servants:

"But when you give to the needy, do not let your left hand know what your right hand is doing, so that your giving may be a secret. Then your Father, who sees what is done in secret, will reward you." (Matthew 6:3-4)

Am I trying to draw attention to myself? Am I doing my service quietly?

God grant that I may be a humble servant.

The quieter the better.

February 7

> *"But when you pray, do not be like the hypocrites, for they love to pray standing in the synagogues and on the street corners to be seen by men. . . . When you pray, go into your room, close the door and pray to your Father, who is unseen."*—MATTHEW 6:5–6

It's a new day for us.

No more the show-off, if that's what we have been.

We learn how to tend to our own business, including our prayers.

We learn to be quietly alone with God.

We learn to find spiritual renewal and rest through quiet meditation and prayer.

We learn to gain new strength for the day, by sharing our concerns privately with the Lord, waiting quietly for the Lord to guide and direct.

We learn that God answers prayer, not as we might wish or desire, but always giving what is best for us. Quietly.

In quietude we find our spiritual renewal and rest, the strength to carry on.

Am I quietly seeking the Lord in prayer? Am I humbly waiting for the Lord to answer?

God grant me the desire for quiet prayer and meditation.

Quiet prayer is powerful prayer.

KEEPING IT SIMPLE

> "And when you pray, do not keep on babbling like pagans, for they think they will be heard because of their many words."—MATTHEW 6:7

Our prayers must remain simple, because recovery is based on simple principles.

The Serenity Prayer and the Lord's Prayer, for the most part, are enough—even more than we are readily able to digest and live.

We may feel uncomfortable about our underdeveloped spirituality, which many equate with not being able to come up with a lot of words.

The truth is that when we come before God, with a humble and contrite heart, there is no need for words at all.

Besides, the Lord knows the secrets of our hearts.

So it's helpful to be keep our prayers as simple as possible, and let God do the leading.

Am I keeping my prayers simple? Am I asking God to lead me?

God grant that I may keep my living and praying simple.

God knows what we need before we ask.

February 9

BLESSING THE NAME OF THE LORD

> *"This is how you should pray: 'Our Father in heaven,
> hallowed be your name.' "*—MATTHEW 6:9

While using, we were far away from God, and
many of us had given up all hope of ever being near
to God.

For if there were a God, then how could this God
permit so much suffering in the world—ours in-
cluded?

And how could we have had so many "bad deals"?
And where was God when we really needed help?

But now things are changing for us. Now we are
ready to lift up the the name of the Lord, who has
lifted us out of the pits and brought us into the light
of a new day.

What a difference!

Now we have this shared experience of recovery
that we are able to share with one another with joy.
Now we are able to pray, "Our Father."

Am I blessing the name of the Lord with my life?
Am I living in gratitude to God?

*God grant that I may bless and lift up the name of
the Lord in my life.*

Nothing can ever be more important for our sobriety
than reverence.

TURNING IT OVER

> *"Your kingdom come, your will be done on earth as it is in heaven."*—MATTHEW 6:10

Before we sobered up and got into our program, our prayer went this way: "My kingdom come. My will be done . . . in heaven as I am doing it right here."

Yes, we were in control, so we thought—in control and the center of the universe.

Now, however, we have come to see that in no way dare we try to run the world any more. To do so is not only dangerous; it is fatal.

Trying to run the world again will only get us running again for the bottle.

Our most productive alternative is to live the prayer, "Your kingdom come, your will be done."

This is the sure way to stay sober and grow spiritually: Leave it up to God to run the world, and pay close attention to the details assigned to each one of us.

Am I praying for God's kingdom to come? Am I praying for God's will to be done?

God grant that I may turn my life over to the Lord.

The kingdom of God comes of itself as we take care of our assigned details.

February 11

LIVING ONE DAY AT A TIME

"Give us today our daily bread."—MATTHEW 6:11

Most of us remember what it was like to be without booze, and the terror of election day—the day when the liquor stores were locked.

Planning to have sufficient supplies in stock required a lot of time, energy, and anxiety.

But with sobriety this changes.

Before sobriety it was our spoken or unspoken prayer to be well supplied, not just for today, but for tomorrow and forever.

That's what heaven would be—a well-stocked cellar filled with high-quality labels on beautiful bottles filled to overflowing.

Now, however, we are urged to pray for only one day at a time of sobriety and for all the needs of life.

Our program is based on "one day at a time" simply because that is all any of us can handle and all we need be concerned about.

Just as our Lord says.

Am I satisfied with one day at a time? Am I praying to live one day at a time?

God grant that I may live my life—one day at a time.

Life cannot be lived beyond today. Life can only be lived today.

RELEASING RESENTMENTS AND GRUDGES

"Forgive us our debts as we also have forgiven our debtors."—MATTHEW 6:12

Complete.
Finished.
Done.

God's forgiveness of our sins leaves us with the obligation and privilege to release ourselves and others from our resentment, to give up, to surrender to the loving forgiveness of the Lord.

When we let go of our resentments, we are released to do something more constructive with our lives than carrying grudges.

We are released to release, to forgive as we are forgiven, to experience a new freedom from the bondage of self.

The truth is that we can't stay sober carrying grudges.

Am I forgiving as I am being forgiven? Am I releasing myself from the bondage of resentment and grudges?

God grant that I may release myself from all resentments and grudges.

Hanging on to resentments not only hurts, it kills.

February 13

PRAYING TO BE PROTECTED

"And lead us not into temptation, but deliver us from the evil one."—MATTHEW 6:13

We can be certain that there are going to be times of testing simply because of the stress of everyday life and living.

While the temptation to return to our old way of life lessens, there are temptations to rebuild self-centeredness and self-will, to get our own way, making sure that we are abundantly rewarded with what we think we have coming.

Knowing this about ourselves, we pray, "Lead us not into temptation"—because there always is the danger of a slip, something we surely want to avoid.

When we turn to God for help, we are asking for protection and getting it. And this isn't the same as running and hiding.

No one builds a good and lasting sobriety by running and hiding. We still have to live in the world of stress and temptation. That's why it's important to seek all the help we can get, asking God to protect us from circumstances we are still not able to handle.

Am I aware of temptations to slip and fall? Am I trusting God to protect me?

God grant me the protection from all temptation.

Temptation isn't the pitfall. Falling into it is.

FORGIVING

"For if you forgive men when they sin against you, your heavenly Father will also forgive you."—MATTHEW 6:14

After thirty years in the program, and helping literally thousands of alcoholics into sobriety, a brother dies drunk—admitting that he couldn't let go of his resentment over having been replaced as the head of an alcohol treatment center that he had built over a period of years.

His friends did everything they could to urge him back into sanity and sobriety, but he simply said, "I can't let go of my resentment."

And, after more than thirty years of apparent sobriety, he died drunk.

In the process of being the great hope for others, our brother had not paid close enough heed to himself.

To stay sober we must practice forgiveness even as we are forgiven.

Am I releasing myself from all negative thoughts, words, and deeds? Am I practicing forgiveness?

God grant that I may forgive as I am forgiven.

To forgive is to be released from the bondage of self.

February 15

LETTING GO

> *"But if you do not forgive men their sins, your Father will not forgive your sin."*—MATTHEW 6:15

The way to death is holding on to grudges and resentments.

There is no way to be released—forgiven—until we release ourselves of negative "get even" feelings.

And, there's no way we can overemphasize the danger that comes from holding on to resentment.

Resentment is our most dangerous enemy.

The one word we should always have before us is, "Forgive." For it is through forgiveness and forgiving that we release ourselves for healing and health.

We alcoholics and other abusers are known resenters of self, others, and God. So it is necessary and good to be reminded that if we don't forgive ourselves and others—as God forgives—we are not open to receive forgiveness and are stuck with negative attitudes that can destroy our sobriety.

Am I holding back on forgiveness? Am I letting bygones be bygones?

God grant that I may let bygones be bygones.

Forgiveness comes only through forgiveness.

LOOKING SAD

> *"When you fast, do not look somber as the hypocrites do."*—MATTHEW 6:16

Sometimes we may seek to impress others with the "sacrifices" we are making to maintain our sobriety—especially when we are feeling sorry for ourselves because of everything we *had* to give up.

Of course, this is a negative way of looking at things. But if we are on a dry drunk, we feel negative, hostile, and ungratefully sorry for ourselves. We want others to pay more attention to us, to understand our pain, to feel sorry for us—which doesn't paint a very pretty picture of ourselves.

Let's remember that recovery isn't a sacrifice.

Nor is it an obstacle course calling for a lot of pain.

Rather, recovery is a state of willingness, coupled with acceptance of and surrender to the will of God for our lives and our healing—with good faith, new hope, and gratitude.

Am I trying to get people to feel sorry for me? Am I expecting to be praised for my sobriety?

God grant that I may not try to manipulate others with my sobriety.

Looking sad in our sobriety isn't sobriety. It's torture.

February 17

BEING SATISFIED THAT GOD KNOWS

"*Your Father, who sees . . .* "—MATTHEW 6:18

When we sober up, there is a tendency—sometimes even a deep desire—to have others recognize what we are doing to become better people.

But the truth is that life goes on, without many people showing much interest in us.

When we enter the so-called "normal" world, we may expect to be noticed as changed people who have taken some simple yet monumental steps for which we should get some recognition.

But people are too busy with their own lives and problems to be all that concerned about us.

This may be shocking to our false pride and may even stir up some resentment. But we can begin to comfort ourselves by realizing that God knows.

Am I unhappy with those who do not pay heed to my recovery, who don't tell me that I'm doing great? Am I content to know that God knows and is happy for me?

God grant that I may be content with my sobriety, at peace with myself.

Applause is not the gift of sobriety. Serenity is.

BEING REWARDED QUIETLY

> *"Your Father, who sees what is done in secret, will reward you."*—MATTHEW 6:18

If we listen to those who have a good sobriety and watch them, we will see quietness.

As far as their service work is concerned, such people are private.

It's not important for them to tell anyone what they are doing, because the rewards are coming from deep inside, where no one but God and they can really see.

The rewards for being quietly private are immediate: a good warm feeling; a sense of being OK with ourselves, with others, and with God; a smile that engages others who may wonder where the smile is coming from.

No longer are we are operating from a purely self-centered base that clutters and confuses.

The more quiet and hidden we become, the greater our rewards of faith, hope, love, and serenity.

Am I finding the quiet rewards of sobriety? Am I content with the quiet ways in which God is blessing me?

God grant that I may be at peace with myself.

The reward of really good work comes quietly.

MAINTAINING SPIRITUAL PRIORITIES

> *"Do not store up for yourselves treasures on earth, where moth and rust destroy, and where thieves break in and steal."*—MATTHEW 6:19

We are being called to focus on spiritual things because we are spiritual beings, and our program for recovery is spiritually based.

While we were using, our primary concern was to keep the material substances handy, at our beck and call, so as to provide us with an escape from reality.

But now we are being asked to place our focus elsewhere, to focus on God. This is the direction in which our Lord points us—urging us on, away from false security, away from that which can easily be infiltrated and destroyed.

With sobriety comes new priorities—spiritual priorities. With this also comes indestructible gifts, as long as we pursue them: faith, hope, love, and serenity.

Do I have my priorities where I want them? Am I seeking the kingdom of God?

God grant that I may keep my priorities straight.

Everything depends on the priorities we pursue.

FOCUSING ON LIFE

"The eye is the lamp of the body."—MATTHEW 6:22

For how long were our eyes focused on our supply of liquor and other drugs?

Our eyes could see the price of booze and the location of liquor stores. And with this focus, our personality became twisted, even perverted.

Our souls were pushed aside for sedatives.

But now we are concentrating on something else.

Now we are paying attention to our sobriety, realizing that we must seek what is pure, good, true, what is helpful to our recovery, choosing new life and new hope.

Now we stay out of high-risk situations that may ignite the old fuse again.

Now we realize how important it is to keep our receptors clean, because we will become what we are looking for and what we open ourselves up to.

What we choose to see is what we will be. Jesus is very clear about this, as we shall see tomorrow.

Am I concentrating my attention in the right places? Am I keeping myself focused on a healthy sobriety?

God grant that I may concentrate my attention in the right places.

It's what we choose to see that really counts.

February 21

BEING CLEAR

> *"If your eyes are good, your whole body will be full of light."*—MATTHEW 6:22

If we are looking for goodness, mercy, and understanding, we will become tolerant, accepting, forgiving, and above all, loving.

Our hearts and minds will be clear and open to receive the many mercies of God.

While we were using, it wasn't possible for us to really focus on anything but the bottle. Our primary concern was to get away from the light of God because we were ashamed of ourselves, because we couldn't handle our pain without alcohol and other drugs.

Our life was filled with darkness rather than light, because we were in a spiritual fog and couldn't see clearly.

By keeping our attention focused on Jesus, we can be crystal clear and filled with his light.

Are my eyes clear? Am I being filled with God's light?

God grant that I may be filled with light.

Being filled with God's light is being totally alive.

KEEPING FOCUSED

> *"But if your eyes are bad, your whole body will be full of darkness."*—MATTHEW 6:23

The truth is that relatively few of us remain with our recovery program. Some say only one in ten of us makes it.

This doesn't mean that the program for recovery doesn't work. It simply means that when our focus on God is broken, we are in the dark.

When we turn from our Higher Power, we turn from light to darkness, which means more failure, more anxiety, more depression, sickness, and failures in our relationships.

It also means deterioration of our health and eventually death. That's how great the darkness is.

So it is important to be reminded that when we turn away from light, we are once again in the darkness of despair and death.

Am I turning away from all that would do me harm? Am I keeping my attention focused on God?

God grant that I may keep my attention focused on the light.

Staying spiritually healthy is focusing on the light.

February 23

RESPECTING THE DARKNESS

"If then the light within you is darkness, how great is that darkness!"—MATTHEW 6:23

We know about failure. We have had much experience with it, and also with despair. We may have slipped or seen others slip and fall—even die—as a result of using again.

Maybe we have had dreams in which we suddenly find ourselves drinking or using other drugs. And we wonder what has happened to us.

There is tremendous fear, sorrow, guilt, and shame. We wake up sweating, praying that it isn't so. And we thank God it's only a dream.

But it is also a taste of the terrible darkness we know so well. The darkness of not being able to stop using.

The darkness of not knowing who we are or what we are doing.

We know that darkness and want no more of it.

Do I have a healthy fear of the darkness? Am I watchful of myself and my sobriety?

God grant that I may always fear the slip.

Respecting the darkness is essential for remaining sober.

SERVING ONE MASTER

"No one can serve two masters."—MATTHEW 6:24

The bottle, or some other substance, was our master, and there was room for no other.

But now we can understand what it's like to have another master.

When we get tied up with Christ as strongly as we have been hooked on booze, there is no telling how much light is going to come into our lives, how much beauty and serenity.

But we can't serve two masters. Sobriety is not something that can be divided, a little bit of this and a little bit of that—a little AA, a little reading, a little prayer, a little meditation now and then, a little service.

If we are to stay sober, we must decide who our master is going to be and commit ourselves accordingly.

One master at a time. One day at a time.

Am I serving one master? Is my master the Christ?

God grant that I may serve Christ, my Lord.

We can only have one master at a time, and it's up to us who or what that master shall be.

LOVING ONE MASTER

"He will hate the one [master] and love the other [master]."—MATTHEW 6:24

Hate is a strong word.

We hate our obsessions that lead us into the valleys of death.

With very strong feelings we turn against all obsessiveness and compulsiveness—the doorways to spiritual destruction and death.

Love is an equally strong word, perhaps stronger—especially as it applies to our life of sobriety. For in sobriety we enter a love relationship with ourselves, with others, and with God.

But we cannot be in two places at once—neither with ourselves, with others, or with God. And anyone who tries experiences certain failure.

We cannot serve Christ and the bottle at the same time. We cannot serve our best interests while we are using.

Am I loving one master? Am I accepting Christ as my only master?

God grant that I may love Christ with my whole heart.

Loving Christ is the best we can ever do for ourselves.

BEING DEVOTED TO CHRIST

> *"He will be devoted to the one and despise the other."*
> —MATTHEW 6:24

Despise is a big word. It means "to look down on with contempt or aversion."

Devoted is even bigger: It means "ardent, devout, affectionate, dedicated by a solemn act."

When we devote ourselves to the way of Christ, which is to Christ himself, we automatically "despise" anything within ourselves that is anti-Christ, that is anti-recovery, and hence anti-life.

Of course, we have days when we begin to remember our past behavior, our compulsive activities, the way we stepped on others and did great harm to ourselves. And we despise all of that.

We are not to despise ourselves. To do so is not devotion to Christ. We are to reject all that is not of Christ, now and in time to come. To do so is to gain health, to heal, to be reborn—one day at a time.

Am I turning away from the old life? Am I devoting myself to Christ?

God grant that I may be totally devoted to Christ, my lord.

Being devoted to Christ is being devoted to life.

February 27

LIVING WITH THE ETERNAL EITHER/OR

"You cannot serve both God and Money."—MAT-
THEW 6:24

We were like jugglers: trying to keep too many
balls in the air at the same time, trying to be sober
while using, trying to be honest while lying, trying
to be faithful when unfaithful.

As our program for recovery becomes our top priority, the many balls we have been trying to keep in
the air descend and come to rest.

Now, our allegiance is to Christ, to our sobriety,
to renewed faith, hope, and love.

We have to keep spirituality ahead of materiality,
placing first things first: Christ over all, our sobriety
above all.

We must avoid any urge to manipulate our way
into the false security of money and possessions, for
doing so will deaden our spirituality, lead us away
from Christ, and endanger our sobriety.

Am I trying to serve God and possessions at the same
time? Am I placing my confidence in Christ and the
program for recovery?

God grant that I may serve Christ first.

Sobriety is a matter of either/or.

LIVING BEYOND FEAR

"Do not worry about your life."—MATTHEW 6:25

We hope never to forget what it was like to awaken at three or four o'clock in the morning with the shakes, the sweating, and the horrendous fear, fear so strong we felt it would certainly destroy us.

But the anxiety did not confine itself to those early morning hours. On the contrary: Until we sedated ourselves again, we were always afflicted with fear and anxiety.

And it was desired tranquility that 'kept us using, that made it seemingly impossible for us to stop using.

But now we have stopped using and we still have an amount of worry and fear; it's not like it was, by any means, but it's still there. "Normal worry," like other people have.

Christ speaks to this worry, telling us to drop it, to give it over to him, to let him carry it for us, to trust him with our fears.

Am I trusting Christ with my life? Am I living beyond fear?

God grant me freedom from fear and worry.

Trusting Christ is living beyond fear and worry.

March 1

TRUSTING GOD

> *"Do not worry about your life, what you will eat."*
> —MATTHEW 6:25

Few of us find ourselves in a perpetual state of physical hunger. So why should we fear whether there is going to be enough food?

Nevertheless, wrapped up in our hearts is the anxiety of being left without help—deserted—without resources to sustain our body and life.

We used to drink away such fears, but that is not for us, not now. So we have to follow directives from someone we trust, and Christ tells us not to worry about such things.

Easier said than done? Of course. But that remains our daily task, and we can do it as we continue to turn our wills and our lives over to the care and keeping of God: "Into your hands I commend my spirit."

Am I trusting God? Am I turning my worries over to the Lord?

God grant that I may turn my worries over to the Lord.

Every day that is totally left to Christ is free of fear and anxiety.

BEING REFRESHED

"Do not worry about your life, what you will . . . drink."—MATTHEW 6:25

These words can sound hilarious to us, especially if our minds trail off and back to prior times. Of course we have to be afraid of what we drink. Look what drinking has done to most of us.

But Christ isn't talking about drinking. He is talking about faith.

We are told that Christ is the living water—the water of life, eternal living water, better than the water that came from the rock to the children of Israel, in the wilderness.

Christ provides spiritual water, refreshing and life-giving. And as long as we turn to Christ, we are where we belong, where the most good can be done for our sobriety and life.

Again the lesson is that we don't have to be afraid as long as we are in Christ and Christ is in us.

Am I permitting Christ to refresh my soul? Am I trusting Christ to renew me day by day?

God grant that I may be refreshed by Christ, day by day.

Being refreshed is to get from Christ what we really need when we need it.

March 3

BEING CLOTHED BY GOD

> *"Do not be afraid . . . about your body, what you will wear."*—MATTHEW 6:25

Clothing protects our bodies and generally helps present us to the world the way we would like to be seen.

"Am I going to be acceptable? Are people going to like me? What will they think of me? Am I going to be able to make them see me the way I want to be seen?"

We may dress to impress, but God clothes us differently—with innocence, blessedness, righteousness, faith, hope, love, patience, and well-doing. Of such is the clothing of the purified heart and of a healthy sobriety.

Am I worried about my appearance? Am I trusting God to clothe me?

God grant that I may be clothed in the Spirit of Christ.

When we let God clothe us in the Spirit of Christ, we are truly clothed in holiness, righteousness, and blessedness.

SEEKING WHAT'S BEST

"Is not life more important than food, and the body more important than clothes?"—MATTHEW 6:25

Life had become constricted. We were locked into material things from which we hoped to gain some kind of emotional and spiritual reward, but which always disappointed. For always we were left with the sensation that something was still missing, still wrong.

In short, more of this or that or the other "thing" did nothing to dispel our fears, our isolation, our separation from self, others, and God.

Now we have come into the light of a new life, the light of a new day.

In this new light of new life we have come to see that our basic needs are spiritual, and that life is more than material things, substances, or otherwise.

We have come to affirm that we are spiritual beings and that nothing short of the Spirit-filled life will satisfy.

Am I being filled with the Spirit of God? Am I seeking first what is best for me?

God grant that I may put first things first.

Whatever we put first in our life is what we'll be.

March 5

BELIEVING GOD

> *"Look at the birds of the air; they do not sow or reap or store away in barns, and yet your heavenly Father feeds them. Are you not much more valuable than they?"*—MATTHEW 6:26

We still have our insecurities. Sobriety doesn't immediately erase old feelings of fear, frustration, and anxiety. We still worry about the present and the future, about what is going to happen to us—whether we are going to be taken care of.

But now we are conscious of our value to God—that God cares for us very deeply, that God is looking out for us.

In our third step of recovery we "make a decision" to turn our wills and our lives over to the care and keeping of God.

Now, however, we must practice believing God—"turning it over" each and every day, in the morning when we awaken, at night before going to sleep.

Am I working my program every day? Am I believing that God takes care of me?

God grant that I may be a believer.

God takes care of us—no matter what.

Living a New Freedom

"Who of you by worrying can add a single hour to his life?"—MATTHEW 6:27

Did we ever catch ourselves trying to do the impossible? Like running the universe. Like making sure that we would never suffer pain, that we would never have to fail at anything we tried.

And then didn't we get so far out in front of ourselves that it was absolutely impossible to get organized and back in control?

Then the sobering time came when someone said that, like it or not, we have no power over the future; there are some things over which we have no control.

Now, however, we have the promise of God that we need not worry, nor even be concerned, because God is in control, and everything is going to come out the way God means it to be, for our benefit and the benefit of others.

No longer need we be enslaved to fear and anxiety.

Am I letting go of the future? Am I living one day at a time with my trust in the Lord?

God grant that I may be set free from anxiety about the future.

There is no greater waste than worry.

March 7

SEEING AND BELIEVING

"See how the lilies of the field grow. They do not labor or spin."—MATTHEW 6:28

We are asked to look outside of ourselves, as well as inside. But sometimes we forget either or both, and simply stop looking, stop seeing.

What we need most is to remember how God is working in the world. Things are being taken care of, even without our doing, simply by God's abundant grace, which clothes the lilies of the field and takes care of us.

Others who are recovering with us in the program can help us look and see. In each other we can see how God is watching out for us, how the miracle of sobriety works.

We can find a great source of hope in the miraculous that's being enacted in and through our recovering brothers and sisters, who once were just as hopeless as we were.

Am I looking at the miracles of God? Am I seeing what God is doing?

God grant that I may see miracles at work in the world and in my life.

Seeing is believing—when we are ready.

SEEKING WHAT'S BEST

> *"But seek first God's kingdom and his righteousness, and all these things will be given you as well."*—MATTHEW 6:33

Contrary to what a lot of people believe or want to believe, God does not specialize in giving us everything we think we need.

But we do get all that we really need, all that is beneficial for our spiritual growth and development.

In fact, we very likely will be getting a lot of the same old stuff, minus the booze or drugs, which may not seem all that inviting.

Happily, however, there is a new component.

No longer are our lives out of control.

Now God is in control.

By seeking what is best, we receive so much more than we could have hoped for.

Am I seeking first the kingdom of God for my life? Am I tasting the goodness of God and giving thanks?

God grant that I may seek what is best for me.

Putting God first must come first.

March 9

FORGOING JUDGMENT

"Do not judge, or you too will be judged."—MAT-
THEW 7:1

While we were using, most of us did our share of
judging and blaming others—for the sad state of
affairs at home, in the nation, and the world. Someone else was responsible for what was going wrong
for us and with us.

There were just too many "stupid people out
there."

Even when we were trying to be liberal in acceptance and forgiveness, down deep in our hearts there
was resistance: fear, anger, and resentment, which
we tried to heap on others, bringing judgment
against them.

Our self-image was low, so we judged others. It
was too painful to deal with ourselves and our own
condition.

Now we know that judging must stop. We must
take care of ourselves and leave others alone

Am I forgoing judgment? Am I accepting myself and
others as we are?

God grant me acceptance of myself and others.

Unloading on others doesn't allow us to unload ourselves.

JUDGING AND BEING JUDGED

> *"For in the same way you judge others, you will be judged."*—MATTHEW 7:2

There's a law of nature that says we get back what we dish out. And haven't we found this to be true?

There is nothing vindictive about this law. In fact, it is very fair and trustworthy. We never have to worry about being cheated by it.

"With the judgment you pronounce you will be judged, and the measure you give will be the measure you get."

This is why, in our program, we continue to take personal inventories, to keep up on what is happening to us.

Negatives beget negatives, resulting in resentment and other inner conflict that threatens our sobriety.

So it's important to go over our feeling states on a regular program of inventory control because this law is always operating, just as Jesus says.

Am I refraining from judging others? Am I staying with my own problems and programs?

God grant that I may never judge others.

There are some things in life we can really count on, like getting back what we dish out.

March 11

STAYING ON OUR OWN CASE

> *"Why do you look at the speck of sawdust in your brother's eye and pay no attention to the plank in your own eye?"*—MATTHEW 7:3

Why is it so easy to see the character defects in others while being hazy or blind about our own? Are we unable to look more closely at ourselves because we are afraid of what we might find?

Generally, those who are always seeing evil in others are also avoiding their own character defects.

Recovery demands that we get to work on our own character defects and sins, face up to them, leave others to themselves and to the Lord, and do not attempt to change them.

We are where we are, not because of defects in others, but because of our own defects, our own disease, our own actions. We have all the work we can possibly do simply to take care of what has to be done in order to improve ourselves.

Am I staying off the defects in others? Am I seeing and accepting my own character defects and working with them?

God grant that I may stay on my own case.

If we have to take a personal inventory, it's appropriate to start with our own.

TAKING CARE OF OURSELVES

> *"How can you say to your brother, 'Let me take the speck out of your eye,' when all the time there is a plank in your own eye?"*—MATTHEW 7:4

Trying to correct someone else, when we need so much corrective work done in our own lives, is an exercise in futility.

The truth is that we have no capability to change others by pointing out their character defects.

And yet we may find ourselves doing just that, trying to change others—even though our program never asks for this, not even in the twelfth Step.

All we can do is carry the message, telling others about our situation: what it was like, what it is like now, how God has worked miracles in our own lives and continues to do so.

This is a far cry from trying to take the speck out of someone else's eye when there is so much to be done to clear our own log jams.

Am I respecting the rights of others to take care of themselves? Am I working with my own character defects?

God grant that I may take care of myself.

The place to work is with the work that is closest to us.

March 13

BEING HONEST

> "You hypocrite, first take the plank out of your own eye, and then you will see clearly to remove the speck from your brother's eye."—MATTHEW 7:5

Healthy sobriety cannot tolerate dishonesty and deceitfulness.

The most destructive character defect is wearing a mask, trying to be what we aren't; trying to get others to see the mask rather than seeing who we really are and what we really are about.

There's no way to stay sober and hypocritical at the same time, as anyone who has had a slip will affirm.

Hiding behind masks, which is hypocrisy, only serves to get us into deeper trouble with ourselves and others.

Sobriety depends on our willingness and capacity to stay with our own program.

Honesty with humility is the key to healthy sobriety, coupled with acceptance and surrender, accepting ourselves the way we are, and surrendering to our need for God's help.

Am I wearing a mask of hypocrisy? Am I being honest with myself, with others, with God?

God grant that I may be absolutely honest.

Hypocrisy is the open doorway to self-destruction.

ASKING

"*Ask.*"—MATTHEW 7:7

When we come into the program of recovery, we must come with an attitude of asking—for help, guidance, encouragement, direction, fellowship, support.

Some of us came into the program against our will, not asking for help, but complaining.

Until there was a reversal in this attitude, we were on very slippery ground.

Until we learned to ask, we were certain to be uncomfortable, if not downright miserable.

Asking for help is something many or most of us have not learned to do very well.

Asking has been equated with helplessness, but that should be acceptable, because we are weak, powerless over alcohol, for instance.

So we start our program by asking: "God grant me the serenity to accept the things I cannot change, the courage to change the things I can, and the wisdom to know the difference."

Am I humbly asking for the help I need? Am I expecting to receive what is necessary to keep my sobriety?

God grant that I may ask for the help I need.

God helps those who ask for help.

ASKING AND RECEIVING

"Every one who asks receives."—MATTHEW 7:8

If we ask God for the blessing of sobriety, we will receive. We do not know when or how the blessing will come, but it will come.

Some of us prayed for years, "Please Lord, help me not to drink any more." And for years there seemed to be no answer, even while the answer was being worked out.

Perhaps we had to keep on asking in order to help build our sincerity, willingness, acceptance, and surrender—the necessary components for a lasting sobriety.

Now that we have tasted the fruits of asking, we see that simple daily prayers are very good for our souls and recovery.

For when we are willing to ask, to ready ourselves for God's answer, the answer finally is given—most often in helpful ways we could not have imagined.

All we have to do is to humbly receive what is being offered.

Am I going to God in prayer? Am I receiving God's blessings into my life each and every day?

God grant me the humility to ask in order to receive.

Asking and receiving go hand in hand, in that order.

SEEKING

"*Seek.*"—MATTHEW 7:7

We must seek sobriety if we are to find it. And although sobriety comes as an act of grace, it cannot be experienced by the uninvolved.

Only seekers can recover, those who go looking for better ways to improve their lives.

Seeking a new life of faith, hope, and love is the excitement and enthusiasm of sobriety.

We have to make an investment of our time and energy to experience the rewards of sobriety.

We have to take steps and make moves, not with the power of our wills, but under the grace of God— seeking sobriety as if it were a hidden treasure.

As long as we are seekers, as long as we pursue spiritual enlightenment, our sobriety will be maintained and strengthened.

Am I diligently seeking the spiritual life? Am I steadfastly seeking to maintain a new life of sobriety?

God grant that I may always be a seeker.

Seeking is the new excitement that comes with sobriety, the new high.

March 17

FINDING

"He who seeks finds."—MATTHEW 7:8

The more we seek spiritual renewal, the more of God's Holy Spirit we find awaiting us, the more exciting recovery becomes—day by day.

We begin to find things we never expected—in the beauty of nature, the warmth of friendship, the support of friends, in the capacity to deal with expected and unexpected problems as they present themselves.

We receive tastes of peace and a sense of well-being for which our hearts have longed.

We find the serenity we are looking for as long as we continue the quest—continue working the program, reading our books, going to meetings, and carrying the message to those who still suffer.

When we honestly ask, God honestly answers.

Am I doing what is required to stay sober, at peace with myself, with others, and with God? Am I finding serenity in the working of my program?

God grant me serenity of spirit.

Serenity is the elusive treasure, belonging to those who seek it.

KNOCKING

> *"Knock."*—MATTHEW 7:7

To maintain a healthy sobriety we must keep at it, not as a drudgery, but as an exciting desire to be healthy.

However, in the course of working our recovery we will have low times, times when we have fallen away from our program, times when we have stopped doing the steps.

In order to get back into the flow of recovery, we must ask, seek, and knock. We must state our renewed desire and intention to be spiritually, emotionally, and physically sober.

In short, it means that we must come to the Lord in prayer. It means knocking on the door. It means exerting ourselves toward God.

Am I faithfully working my program? Am I exerting myself toward God?

God grant that I may exert myself in your direction.

Sobriety is going for help wherever it is offered.

March 19

> *"To him who knocks, the door will be opened."*
> —MATTHEW 7:8

If we continue in our program for recovery—be it AA or other helpful recovery programs—positive things happen. Doors open that once were closed to us.

In many cases this includes new openings between ourselves and others: wives, husbands, parents, children, and other associates.

Once we are involved in the honest venture and adventure of sobriety, our environment begins to change. People begin to notice that we are changing, and they begin to treat us differently.

As we progress in the working of our program, we see more open doors and begin walking through them, into the promises and blessings of a good and lasting sobriety.

Am I seeing open doors? Am I walking through them?

God grant that I may see the doors that are open to me and walk through them.

Sobriety is the open door to new life, new hope, and new joy.

TREATING OTHERS AS OURSELVES

"In everything, do to others what you would have them do to you."—MATTHEW 7:12

When it comes to our sobriety, we need all the help we can get—all of the "community" available to us: with the church, family, friends in AA, and other support groups.

In this sense recovery is a community project, each of us helping the other along the way, lending support, giving assistance as needed, giving ourselves to others, as we would have them give to us.

The founders of AA based the entire program for recovery on the belief that one cannot stay sober unless one also is generous.

From firsthand experience we discover that if we treat others the way we want to be treated, the program works, and we stay sober.

Am I treating others the way I want to be treated? Am I being of help to others who suffer?

God grant that I may be of service to others and of service to myself.

We are of no help to ourselves until we are of help to others.

March 21

WALKING A NARROW PATH

> *"Enter through the narrow gate. For wide is the gate and broad is the road that leads to destruction, and many enter through it."*—MATTHEW 7:13

We were rigid in our attitudes, our mind-sets, our dedication to a destructive way of life.

There was nothing we couldn't do when properly lit up.

Most of us kept on using after being warned that we were destroying ourselves.

We knew no discipline. We were strong-minded. We refused to walk the straight and narrow. We tried, and often succeeded in all but destroying ourselves.

However, some of us didn't destroy ourselves. Some of us found the narrow gate, and even began to discipline ourselves, walking the straight and narrow way that leads to life.

Am I seeing the narrow gate? Am I choosing to walk through it?

God grant that I find the narrow gate and walk through it.

The narrow way is not the way of a closed mind, but of a sane one.

STAYING WITH THE STRUGGLE

> *"But small is the gate and narrow the road that leads to life, and only a few find it."*—MATTHEW 7:14

"With so much turmoil, trouble, and confusion, who needs any more of it?" That's precisely what we decided when we were using.

We decided that there was no sense struggling with pain as long as there were pain killers available.

Our capacity to experience honest feelings was anesthetized.

Now, however, with a growing sobriety, we are discovering that we can walk a straighter path, in spite of our insecure feelings of fear, anger, and resentment.

Now we no longer find it necessary to run and hide from problems that beset all people.

Now we are able to walk the narrow road of honesty, courage, and integrity that leads to new life, new hope, and new joy.

Am I dealing with my pain? Am I working with my difficulties in positive ways?

God grant that I may stay with the struggle.

Life is a series of struggles to be faced and problems to be solved.

March 23

BEING ALERT

> *"Watch out for false prophets. They come to you in sheep's clothing."*—MATTHEW 7:15

The biggest false prophet is the one inside ourselves; the one that says, "One drink won't make a difference. One drink won't kill you."

Periodically, so-called "scientific studies" try to establish that some "alcoholics" can return to social drinking. Certainly, many have tried.

From within and without come the false prophets, yet we are our own most deadly false prophet of all: "Maybe I'm cured. Maybe I never really was one in the first place. Maybe I'm not right now—an alcoholic, a dope addict, a food freak."

When such feelings and thoughts come to us— and they come to all of us sooner or later—it is time to get to a meeting, time to call a sponsor, to talk to someone; time to make a twelfth-Step call on ourselves and someone else.

Am I paying attention to my sobriety? Am I listening to strange voices about myself?

God grant that I listen not to false prophets.

When in doubt, take a deep breath and say a prayer.

BEING HONEST AND UPRIGHT

"By their fruit you will recognize them."—MATTHEW 7:16

What seems so obvious has not always been clear, especially for those of us who wanted others to believe our lies. And we couldn't understand those who refused to take us at our word.

While we expected others to toe the line, to show us who they were by what they did, we held to no such accounting for ourselves.

We became self-righteously angry when someone suggested or vaguely intimated that we too should be held to the rigorous standard: "By their works you shall know them."

We do not have to know what others are doing with their lives. Rather, we have to pay close attention to what we actually are doing with ourselves, trying to be honest and upright.

Am I doing what is honest and upright? Am I being seen for what I want to be?

God grant that I may be true to myself, doing what is honest and upright.

Being honest and upright is what makes the real difference.

March 25

BEING WHAT WE ARE MEANT TO BE

"Do people pick grapes from thornbushes, or figs from thistles?"—MATTHEW 7:16

Finally the truth began to dawn: Like it or not, we would have to change, if for no other reason than that we had nowhere else to go with the exercise and extension of our character defects.

People were running out of energy to deal with us. Emotionally and spiritually we separated ourselves from others and God.

No longer could we afford to play games with reality, or run from it, without totally destroying ourselves.

The time finally came for God to uproot the thorns and thistles of our lives, replacing them with plantings from the garden of God—with faith, hope, and love.

Am I becoming a new creature in Christ? Am I bearing the new fruit of righteousness, innocence, and blessedness?

God grant that the thorns and thistles be gone, that new hope be given.

It is in becoming what we have been created to be that life takes on the true dimensions of joy.

BEING CHANGED

> *"Every good tree bears good fruit, but a bad tree bears bad fruit."*—MATTHEW 7:17

We became more isolated, alone, misunderstood, lonely, overlooked, forgotten, cheated, and persecuted. So it seemed.

The disease was progressing, slowly but surely, day by day—eating away at us, emotionally, physically, and spiritually.

We didn't understand what was happening to us, that we were growing progressively more ill.

There was a growing loss of soundness.

It became increasingly clear that nothing good could come from our lives, the way we were attempting to live them.

Then, one miraculous day, we began to change. What was so bad began to turn around. What was good began to happen. All because something inside ourselves had been miraculously redirected by God's power.

Am I changing? Am I getting better day by day?

God grant that I may bear the good fruits of sobriety—of faith, hope, and love.

Daybreak always comes after darkness.

March 27

ESCAPING THE FIRE THAT BURNS

"Every tree that does not bear good fruit is cut down and thrown into the fire."—MATTHEW 7:19

While we are using we are doing it to ourselves— throwing our lives away. It's like a mathematical equation. We can't change the laws by which this disease operates: feed the disease and you become increasingly enmeshed in confusion and mounting despair.

We chose not to be aware of the finality with which we were dealing, because it was far too frightening.

But there was no changing the course of events as long as we were enslaved.

We didn't want to, nor were we able to, admit the calamity in which we were involved.

We attempted to dress things up, to color reality to fit our own wishes and desires.

However, the "fire" not only was left burning within, but we also were fueling the flames, giving up our bodies and souls to be burned.

Am I taking good care of myself? Am I escaping the fire that burns?

God grant that I may not cast myself into the fire.

Working on sobriety is the primary task, one day at a time

Entering the Kingdom

> *"Not everyone who says to me 'Lord, Lord,' will enter
> the kingdom of heaven, but only he who does the will
> of my Father."*—MATTHEW 7:21

We found out—most of us because of severe set-
backs—that getting sober was more than crying,
"Lord! Lord!" even though we didn't know what
that "something more" was.

Then, one day, we began to discover that acceptance was the needed gift.

Then, through a miracle of grace we began to let
go and let God. With this came a sense of profound
relief.

We became honest with ourselves, with others,
and with God.

We entered the kingdom of God.

We began to breathe the breath of new life.

Am I accepting my condition for what it is? Am I
surrendering myself to the will and power of God for
me and my life?

*God grant that I may have new life today in accept-
ance and surrender.*

Actions speak louder than words, something we all
know but aren't always ready to believe.

BUILDING ON FIRM FOUNDATIONS

> *"Every one who hears these words of mine and puts them into practice is like a wise man who built his house on the rock."*—MATTHEW 7:24

Perhaps there were concerned friends who were worried about the course of our destructive lives, and maybe some of them said too much to us in their anxiety. Be that as it may, whatever the circumstances, we had closed off the "still, small voice" of God.

We were not able to follow directions, to do for ourselves what was best.

Due to circumstances beyond our control, we finally came to see and accept the need to listen to the voice of our Higher Power—to recover, to lead a sober life.

We began building our lives upon a rock foundation, rather than on shifting sand. And that foundation we began to call, "sobriety."

Am I building on a firm foundation? Am I hearing the voice of the Lord in my life?

God grant me a firm foundation.

Getting to work on the foundation is where we have to begin each day.

BEING SECURED

> *"The rain came down, the streams rose, and the winds blew and beat against that house; yet it did not fall, because it had its foundations on the rock."*—MATTHEW 7:25

Happily, and not too far into our new life of sobriety, we began to sense a firmer foundation on which to build our faith, hope, and life.

For many of us this meant a new relationship to Christ.

No longer was Christ a nonperson, a nonentity. Rather, he became what we had longed for all the days we had been using: our savior.

We had set ourselves on a foundation that could not be shaken, and that Rock is Christ.

And our house did not fall. Neither could it be washed away.

Am I keeping my foundation secured on Christ? Am I secured in the Lord?

God grant that I may keep my foundation secured in Christ, my Lord.

Christ Jesus is the foundation that cannot be shaken or destroyed.

March 31

REMAINING FAITHFUL

> *"But every one who hears these words of mine and does not put them into practice is like a foolish man who built his house on sand. The rain came down, the streams rose, and the winds blew and beat against that house, and it fell with a great crash."*—MATTHEW 7:26–27

If we don't process ourselves in health-giving ways, the foundations of our lives shift and shudder.

Then even the smallest of storms can bring us into areas of great danger, as we become disconnected from our support systems.

There's no doubt that we are going to be confronted with many trials that can endanger our sobriety.

Therefore it's doubly important for us to remain faithful to our program, taking all necessary precautions, keeping ourselves firmly grounded in our program of sobriety and growth.

Am I remaining faithful to my program for recovery? Am I avoiding shaky foundations?

God grant that I may remain faithful in the working of my program.

It's what's underneath us that really counts.

BEING READY AND WILLING

"I will go and heal him."—MATTHEW 8:7

As we discover in the working of our program, our need is for healing, and healers.

Often it is rightfully said that "recovery is a community affair," with each of us bringing healing gifts and insights to the other, the Christ in us to the Christ in them.

The Lord works through other people; the healing and life-giving Christ in them reaches out and touches the healing and life-giving Christ in us.

Our challenge of faith is to remember and believe that the Lord is willing and able to heal, as long as we are ready and willing to be helped.

This is not an arbitrary matter. Rather, it is a simple truth: Until we are willing to be healed, there can be no healing.

However, when we are willing, when we are ready to ask for help, it is the Lord who says, "I will come and heal."

Am I ready to be healed? Am I asking the Lord to heal me?

God grant that I may always be ready to be healed.

Being ready and willing is the open door to healing and health.

April 2

BEING TOUCHED AND HEALED

"He touched her hand and the fever left her, and she got up and began to wait on him."—MATTHEW 8:15

Then, one day, it was over. That special time came—that day, hour, moment when we were able to say, "No more. I have had enough. I can't go on this way any longer."

It was as though someone touched us and the fever left us, and we were able to rise and live and serve.

And this is the way it has happened for hundreds and thousands, even millions of recovering people:

Hopeless and dead one day, alive and growing the next.

Enslaved, and miraculously set free.

The Lord touched us, and the fever left.

And, thanks be to God, the Lord is always willing to touch us again and again, to heal us.

Am I allowing Christ to touch me each and every day? Am I allowing myself to be healed?

God grant that I may be touched and healed again and again and again.

Only as we are touched by the healing hand of God are we given new life, hope, and joy.

BEING ACCEPTED AND FORGIVEN

> *"He took up our infirmities and carried our diseases."*
> —MATTHEW 8:17

Many of us carry the "infirmity" of shame and guilt.

We need to be understood and accepted.

We need the affirmation of a Higher Power—someone who knows precisely where we are with ourselves, who understands our failings and short-comings better than we do—who knows our pain, having endured it.

Christ is that person, having taken upon himself our infirmities and diseases—our sins and shortcomings. Christ knows and understands what we are and where we are coming from. We are no mystery to him. And Christ accepts us just the way we are, with no questions asked.

Am I allowing the Lord to minister to my deep need for forgiveness? Am I turning over my guilt and shame to the Lord?

God grant that I may place my faith and hope in Christ.

With Christ there is acceptance and forgiveness, no matter what we have been.

April 4

MAKING DECISIONS

> *"Follow me, and let the dead bury their own dead."*
> —MATTHEW 8:22

Healthy sobriety is a program of action based on decision making.

Although we may have a longing to stay sober, nothing begins to happen, for the better until we make a decision to stop using. It's as simple as that.

There was a man who said he wanted to follow Jesus, but said he couldn't do so until his father died. To which Jesus said, "Let the dead bury the dead."

Sometimes sobriety is that radical—leaving all behind, pressing on toward the goal, deciding to do what has to be done to stay sober, to live a productive life.

Am I willing to be responsible for my own life? Am I accepting personal responsibility for my life and the living of it?

God grant that I may make a decision to accept personal responsibility for my life and the living of it.

"Forgetting what is behind, I press on toward the goal." (Philippians 3:13–14)

CLEARING FEAR

> *"You of little faith, why are you so afraid?"*—MAT-
> THEW 8:26

Even while using, we had an element of faith. But in what?

Each time we took a drink, or popped a pill, we expected to be less fearful and more comfortable with ourselves, with others, even more comfortable with the universe.

But then came the aftermath, the trembling and shaking, the fear. Our faith had been misplaced—the faith we had in the bottle, in the fix.

Now, however, we are learning to place our faith where it will do some good, as our faith in God grows, little by little, day by day.

The more we place our trust and confidence in the redemptive and healing power of Christ, the more our fear lessens.

Christ helps us overcome our lack of faith and our fears.

Am I placing my faith in Christ? Is my fear lessening?

God grant me faith in Christ, to overcome my fear.

Faith in Christ clears the way for a life beyond fear.

April 6

TAKING HEART IN FORGIVENESS

> *"Take heart, Son; your sins are forgiven."*—MATTHEW 9:2

We must have assurance about the forgiveness of sins, because so much has gone wrong with us and so many wrongs need to be righted.

That's why we work the steps, searching out our character defects and making amends. We confess to ourselves, to another human being, and to God the exact nature of our wrongs.

But we need more.

We need to be assured, by someone who has the authority, that our sins are forgiven.

Those whom we have offended may forgive, and we may forgive ourselves; but the feelings of guilt, shame, and remorse often remain.

But, thanks be to God, there is total and absolute forgiveness through Christ who gives himself to and for us—with all of our transgressions—for every wrong we ever have done.

Do I believe that God has forgiven my sins? Have I forgiven myself?

God grant that I may believe that my sins are all forgiven.

Forgiveness is the release of ourselves to God, who releases us to live abundantly

RETURNING TO START OVER

"Get up, take your mat and go home."—MATTHEW 9:6

By some miraculous power, greater than ourselves, we find ourselves rising above the desire to use.

What once was impossible has been accomplished.

The time comes for us to rise and go home. Time to return to neglected places and people, and to our own neglected self.

The "return" can be frightening because there are places we don't remember, which have been blocked and blacked out. Fogged in.

We may hope that others will receive us with joy and laughter. But it doesn't always turn out that way.

To "rise and go home" may be very frightening, but the Spirit is able to lead us, and Christ is always ready to walk by our side, pointing the way.

Am I willing to rise up? Am I ready to start over?

God grant that I may not be afraid of dealing with things as they are.

Sooner or later we must go back in order to move on with our lives.

April 8

BEING LED

"Follow me."—MATTHEW 9:9

Without help we will find ourselves slipping back into confusion, into "stinking thinking." And with this comes the danger of relapse.

Early in our program we are urged to get a sponsor, to find someone who can lead us through the very difficult and demanding steps toward recovery.

For the truth is that when we come into the program, we cannot find our way without help. We are too confused, too out of it. We know so little because we have been so blind, so spiritually bound.

Fortunately, for those who are disposed to be led, there is Christ, who is ready to lead and guide, Christ who uses our sponsors to help us along the way.

If we are to stay sober, we must find in ourselves a "following" attitude—following the sound leading of a good sponsor, and most of all, the leading of our Lord.

Am I paying close attention to my sobriety? Am I allowing myself to be led?

God grant that I may allow myself to be led, day by day.

Getting a good sponsor is a first order of business.

BEING MERCIFUL

> *"But go and learn what this means: 'I desire mercy, not sacrifice.' "*—MATTHEW 9:13

Somewhere in our days of using there came the longing for mercy. We were unable to help ourselves be straight, and getting drunk was becoming more painful with each passing day.

Many of us were already asking God for mercy: "Lord, please help me stop!"

But, for a time, perhaps even longer than we wished, the pain continued.

No matter how messed up, how shaky, how physically and emotionally beaten, how sorrowful and sad and repentant we were, it all started again. More self-induced punishment.

Mercy was being offered but we couldn't see it, couldn't make use of it, until that day when a miracle happened, when mercy took; when we stepped out into the sunlight of a new day of freedom.

Am I grateful for the mercy of God given to me? Am I being merciful to others who suffer?

God grant that I may be merciful, as mercy has been given to me.

Being merciful is the first act of gratitude.

ACCEPTING SALVATION

> *"I have not come to call the righteous, but sinners."*
> —MATTHEW 9:13

With Christ everything is contrary to the ways of the world.

For instance, Christ Jesus came to be with and to save sinners, rather than to be with and save those who see themselves as being righteous, with no need for salvation.

This should be heartening, because we know we are sinners who had hit the skids and bottomed out, in a place where there seemed to be no hope and no salvation.

But we began to sense that we were being called to a new way of life: a life of faith, hope, love, and joy.

We began to understand that Christ came to us not because we were straight, honest, righteous, and good, but because we were helplessly mired down and lost.

Do I believe that Christ came to save sinners? Do I believe that Christ came to save me?

God grant that I may be grateful for my salvation.

Accepting salvation is the step we have always been looking for and wanting to take.

Becoming New People

> *"No one sews a patch of unshrunk cloth on an old garment, for the patch will pull away from the garment, making the tear worse."*—MATTHEW 9:16

Weren't we always trying to patch things up rather than looking for a new way of doing things, of changing our behavior, of becoming new people?

Many times we promised ourselves and others that things were going to be different, that we were going to turn over a new leaf.

It was like trying to put an unshrunk patch into an old garment. When the garment is washed the patch shrinks and the garment doesn't, so the defect is enlarged.

Now, however, we no longer are trying to patch old garments with new patches. Rather, we are asking God to remake us into new creatures.

Am I becoming a new creature in Christ? Am I putting on new spiritual garments rather than patching the old ones?

God grant that I may become a new creature in Christ.

Patchwork simply doesn't work for recovery.

April 12

SEPARATING THE NEW FROM THE OLD

"Neither do men pour new wine into old wineskins. If they do, the skins will burst, the wine will run out and the wineskins will be ruined."—MATTHEW 9:17

We have to watch out that we don't try to fit the new and changing into the old and worn out.

We can't go back to our old ways with our new visions and ambitions for sobriety.

And there are places we must avoid for the sake of our sobriety: drinking places, using places. Whatever it was that helped set us up and off again and again.

No longer dare we invest ourselves in the destructive aspects of the old ways, the old places, and people who are still using.

Neither can we force our new approach to life and living on those who are not ready to receive it.

What is new cannot be poured into what is old and worn.

This is something we must recognize, without any regrets.

Am I trying to blend the new with the old? Am I letting go of all that would cause me to slip and fall?

God grant that I may not try to force the new way of life into the old way of life.

Sobriety is a completely new way of life and living.

INVESTING OURSELVES

> *"They pour new wine into new wineskins, and both are preserved."*—MATTHEW 9:17

What we are looking for each day is newness, freshness, a rebirth of the human spirit. But, of course, not every day will bring such experiences.

Sobriety doesn't promise a new kind of everlasting glow to take the place of former glows.

On the contrary, we find ourselves in many struggles, some of them very frightening and depressing, just as "normal" people do.

Now, however, something new and fresh is pulsing within us: the Spirit of God working in our lives.

And, if we will pay attention to the leading of God, we will be like new wine. We will look for new places to be, and new, healthy relationships.

We place ourselves where new life can be preserved.

Jesus speaks the truth: for something new to be preserved, it must be deposited in a new place.

Am I investing my life where it will do my spirit the most good? Am I doing what is best for my sobriety?

God grant that I may invest my new life in new places.

Let us always be careful about what we do with ourselves.

April 14

HAVING OUR SPIRITUAL EYES OPENED

> *Then he touched their eyes and said, "According to your faith will it be done to you." And their sight was restored.*—MATTHEW 9:29.

As we are touched by the healing hand of Christ, our spiritual eyes are opened. We become more able to see things that once were hidden—things about ourselves, about others, about God and the universe in which we are learning to live.

Now we are beginning to see that each day is a new day with new lessons to be learned, new gifts to be uncovered, new terrain to cross over, and new problems to be solved.

Now we are being touched by the healing hand of God, and now we are beginning to see new life, new hope, and new joy. We are having our spiritual eyes opened.

Are my spiritual eyes being opened to the mercies of God? Am I able to see God's love and to give thanks?

God grant that I am able to see new life, new hope, and new joy.

To be touched by the healing hand of Christ is to have our eyes opened to new life, new hope, new joy.

OFFERING OURSELVES IN SERVICE

> *Then he said to his disciples, "The harvest is plentiful,*
> *but the workers are few. Ask the Lord of the harvest,*
> *therefore, to send out workers into his harvest field."*
> —MATTHEW 9:37–38.

Millions suffer from our disease.

Our Lord expresses deep concern for them, asking us to reach, to touch, to offer whatever help we are able to give, sharing ourselves, telling how it was, how it now is, and how it works, sharing our strength and hope.

Also we are being asked to pray for more willing workers.

Much depends on our willingness to pray, because so much rests on prayer.

The more we pray, the more willing we become to help. And the more help we offer, the more help we receive. In this respect, ours is a very healthy selfish program.

Am I praying for God's help? Am I offering myself in service?

God grant that I may offer myself as a helper to others.

It is in giving that we receive.

April 16

RECEIVING FREELY . . . GIVING FREELY

"Freely you have received, freely give."—MATTHEW
10:8

Once we have our feet planted on the pathway of
sobriety, there is much we can do to help ourselves,
but the help comes from the Lord.

What makes our program work is the fact that we
are all recipients of God's grace. We didn't become
sober because of willpower and sheer determination.
Therefore there is nothing to brag about, even
though we can and should feel very good about ourselves, remembering where we have come from.

Let us always remember that we have received
without paying. Then let us give freely, expecting
nothing in return—other than the joy of knowing
that we are always in the process of repaying an
honest debt, each time we reach out and touch another person who suffers.

Am I giving freely as it has been given to me? Am
I holding back on the gifts I have received?

*God grant that I may give freely of the gifts given to
me.*

Freely giving is the real essence of hope and joy in
sobriety.

LETTING GOD WORK THROUGH US

> *"For it will not be you speaking, but the Spirit of your Father speaking through you."*—MATTHEW 10:20

Most often what we have to give is our own story. But this can be frightening. How to share it?

A rather new soul in the program was called upon to make his first twelfth-step call. At the meeting he shared his concerns with the group and was assured that he would do just fine as long as he was able to listen and, when appropriate, to share his own story.

After the meeting an older member took him aside and with considerable firmness asked, "What are you doing with yourself? Why are you so afraid? Do you think that you are the one who is making this call? Get this straight! You are not the one who is doing the work. God is doing the work through you. And your thinking anything else is a lot of needless worry fed by false pride."

Am I letting God work in and through me? Am I keeping myself out of the way?

God grant that I may let the Spirit work through me and keep myself out of the way.

Keeping ourselves out of the way is one of the greater accomplishments of true sobriety.

April 18

STANDING FIRM

> *"He who stands firm to the end will be saved."*—MAT-
> THEW 10:22

No doubt about it, we must stand firm: not only
to keep our sobriety in process, but for anything else
worthwhile.

Endurance is one of the saintly virtues. Whoever
stands firm until the end will be saved from all sorts
of needless suffering, about which we know so much.

For us endurance is one day at a time.

Our immediate "end" is the end of this day, not
the end of tomorrow or the days to come.

Standing firm has to do with being faithful to
ourselves, maintaining our sobriety—one day at a
time.

Why is this so? Why endurance one day at a time?
Simply because this is all we are capable of doing,
because this is all anyone is capable of doing.

We can stand firm one day at a time.

By so doing, we find our salvation: lasting sobriety,
unity with ourselves, with others, with God.

Am I praying for the gift of endurance? Am I standing firm, one day at a time?

God grant me the gift of endurance, one day at a time.

One day at a time is a whole lifetime.

Maintaining Our Spirituality

"Do not be afraid of those who kill the body but cannot kill the soul."—matthew 10:28

What were we afraid of? Losing those close to us? Losing our jobs, our self-respect, our health, our lives? Who knows?

Can we ever forget how all of the hidden fear came roaring to the surface, buffeting our bodies, causing us to tremble and shake?

Little did we know that there was a greater danger still: We were in the process of losing our connecting links.

Today we know that the greatest loss we can ever experience is not the loss of our bodies, but of our spirituality—our connection with self, with others, and with God.

Keeping these connections is the primary reason for our staying with the program, staying with people who, like ourselves, have known life-threatening fear, but now are on the road to recovery.

Am I paying close attention to my spirituality? Am I staying with my program for recovery?

God grant that I may stay clean and sober today.

Maintaining our spiritual life must always come first.

April 20

BEING AWARE OF GOD'S CARE

> *"Even the very hairs of your head are all numbered."*
> —MATTHEW 10:30

What counts in the long run is that we are being looked after, that someone cares. Because there are bound to be many days of testings, many days of trials and temptations.

Left to ourselves, we slip and fall.

Again and again, we must be reminded that God knows each of us intimately, and that God cares.

By ourselves we never would have been able to take our first sober breath.

Most of us know that to be a fact.

We have come to see and believe that we are being dealt with in detail, as though every aspect of ourselves is known and accounted for by the Lord.

Am I aware of God's loving care? Am I celebrating the love of God in my life?

God grant that I may celebrate the mystery of divine love.

God cares for us more than we care for ourselves.

LOSING AND GAINING

> *"Whoever finds his life will lose it, and whoever loses his life for my sake will find it."*—MATTHEW 10:39

By losing what we once counted on so desperately, we find new life.

So it also is with any other fixations we may have, whether on people, places, or things, including our lives.

Until we are ready to give up, to turn over, to lose whatever it is that binds us to this material world, we are hindering our growth and development as spiritual beings, endangering our sobriety.

Jesus offers us a great opportunity: "He who loses his or her life for my sake will find it."

Thus we are provided with something we actually need—a place to dispose of ourselves and our demanding ego.

By making such a disposition we become truly free human beings, no longer bound and fettered by the demands of our fear and neediness.

Am I losing my life for Christ's sake? Am I finding new life and the joy of living it?

God grant that I may lose my life for Christ's sake in order to find it.

Only by losing can we gain.

GIVING AND GROWING

> *"If anyone gives a cup of cold water . . . because he*
> *is my disciple . . . he will certainly not lose his reward."*
> —MATTHEW 10:42

Now we are being asked to extend our Lord's
compassion to others.

There are some dangers involved here.

The first is that we may extend ourselves so much
outwardly toward others that we lose sight of our
own need for personal attention.

The second is that we become so self-centered in
our sobriety that we lose sight of others who need to
hear the message of recovery, who need attentive
service, with compassion.

But the truth is that we cannot keep our sobriety
unless we extend ourselves in both directions, in-
wardly and outwardly—toward ourselves and toward
others.

Am I giving and growing? Am I being compassionate
toward others who suffer?

God grant that I may give and grow.

Give as it has been given unto you, pressed down and
running over.

BELIEVING AND LIVING THE MIRACLES OF GOD

"The blind receive sight, the lame walk, those who have leprosy are cured, the deaf hear, the dead are raised up, and the good news is preached to the poor."
—MATTHEW 11:5

In spite of the known and experienced miracles of recovery, practicing alcoholics most often look like lost causes to us who are now living sober.

Try as we might, we find it difficult to imagine another person recovering. Yet it is happening every day to hundreds and thousands—many times right in our midst, right before our eyes. We simply have to marvel, as the blind receive their sight, as the lame walk, as the dead are raised up, and the poor have the good news given to them—the good news of sobriety.

Am I believing the miracles of God? Am I seeing the miracles at work in my life and the lives of others?

God grant that I may believe the miracles of recovery, and grow.

Believing and living the miracles of God is our new way of life.

April 24

HEARING AND GROWING

"He who has ears, let him hear."—MATTHEW 11:15

What we missed hearing was the voice of God trying to get through to us.

We didn't hear: "Rarely have we seen a person fail who has thoroughly followed our path into sobriety."

We didn't hear: "Those who do not recover are people who cannot or will not completely give themselves to this simple program."

We didn't hear: "Some of us have tried to hold on to our old ideas and the result was nil until we let go absolutely."

We didn't hear: "But there is One who has all power—that one is God. May you find him now!"

Looking back we can now see that for the most part we were a closed book.

Then, for the first time in our lives, perhaps, we began to drop our defenses to listen and to hear. Even to believe!

Am I listening and believing? Am I hearing and growing?

God grant me the gifts of hearing and growing.

Once we start hearing what God is saying, we are well on our way to recovery.

FINDING REST FOR OUR SOULS

> *"Take my yoke upon you and learn from me, for I am gentle and humble in heart, and you will find rest for your souls."*—MATTHEW 11:29

At first, early on in our using days, it felt as though we were finding rest for our souls as the drink or the pills went down—followed by sensations of rest and calm, and everything going right for us. But this changed for the worse.

While we received temporary relief with our drug of choice, the desired effect soon began to wear off, followed by growing anxiety and depression.

Anything but rest for our souls.

However, once we stopped using, once we began to pay attention to our sobriety, allowing the hidden pain to surface, things began to change for the better. And we began to find rest for our souls.

Am I following Christ? Am I finding rest for my soul?

God grant that I may find rest for my soul, one day at a time.

Following Christ is finding rest for our souls.

April 26

BEING YOKED TO CHRIST

> *"For my yoke is easy and my burden is light."*—MAT-
> THEW 11:30

Jesus promises that when we are yoked to him as servants and coworkers life is easier and burdens are lighter.

We are not promised material prosperity or freedom from the normal course of pain in growth.

Essentially, what is lighter about the yoke and burden of Christ is the will to be honest and straightforward in all things.

No longer do we have to approach life in a bent position. While we still face many painful and difficult problems, life is much easier now.

Being yoked to Christ, we are now able to accept and share the promised redemption of our battered lives, as outlined in the suggested program for recovery—the Twelve Steps.

Am I taking on the yoke of Christ? Are my burdens becoming lighter and easier to bear?

God grant that I may be yoked to Christ.

Being yoked to Christ is much easier on us than being yoked to a bottle.

BEARING GOOD FRUIT

> *"Make a tree good and its fruit will be good, or make a tree bad and its fruit will be bad, for a tree is recognized by its fruit."*—MATTHEW 12:33

No longer are there any in-between places for us to be.

By now, millions of us have decided to go for health, new life, new hope, and new joy—sobriety and recovery.

Once we decided that we wanted to be like a good tree bearing good fruit, things began to change for the better—not radically or spectacularly, but slowly and surely. Like an apple blossom turning into a fine ripening apple, we became God's work in process.

We also came to see and accept the reality that there is no turning back to the old life, if we want to live soberly and grow.

If we want to be good people, we concentrate on doing good things, helping ourselves and others to live.

Am I bearing good fruit? Am I helping myself and others to live and grow?

God grant me the grace to give and to grow.

We are who we choose to be.

GROWING FROM WITHIN

> *"Out of the overflow of the heart the mouth speaks."*
> —MATTHEW 12:34

It's what develops from within that makes the difference, where the real growth takes place.

Simply moving the furniture around is not helpful. We must come up with a new attitude, a more healthful way of looking at life.

Our recovery depends on the grace of God growing and developing from within. We can call this the process of being born again, because that's what it is.

Negativity is being replaced by positive thoughts, words, and deeds. Self-centeredness begins to leave us.

While the old ego (self-centeredness) is fighting to the finish, a new abundance of God's grace is growing within, to be shared with others, as we are becoming new creations of the Lord.

Am I becoming a new creation of the Lord? Am I being filled with the abundance of God?

God grant me new life, hope, and joy.

The growth process always is from the inside to the outside.

HOLDING FAST TO THE GOOD

"The good man brings good things out of the good stored up in him."—MATTHEW 12:35

Who wants to imagine himself or herself as being evil? Yet we have to face and confess our sins in order to develop a new way of life with a healthy sobriety.

We didn't consciously decide to do harm to ourselves and others. It just came out that way as our disease grew and intensified.

We wanted to be good and to bring forth good, but instead we got drunk and launched into behavior patterns that, as we now see, were destructive.

Often we made resolutions to change, even prayed to God for change. But everything remained terribly confusing until we were ready to be changed from within.

That took more than our power and our doing. That called for God's intervention, making it possible for us to bring forth good treasures of new life.

Am I holding fast to the good? Is my life reflecting my deepest values and priorities?

God grant me the goodness that flows from within.

Holding fast to what is good is holding fast to the very best there is for us.

April 30

> *"When an evil spirit comes out of a man, it goes through arid places seeking rest and does not find it."*
> —MATTHEW 12:43

Suddenly, miraculously, the need and desire to use was abated, to the extent that we didn't have to do it any more.

We were left with empty places in our lives.

We also discovered that the "unclean spirits" (as we can easily call them) do not leave without a struggle, nor are they willing to be displaced beings.

Now our greatest danger is that we will neglect our program, passing lightly over the need to have empty places filled.

Now we must be spiritually filled with the mercies of God, leaving no room for further possessions by those forces beyond our control.

Now we must avoid slips, at all costs.

Am I setting myself up for a slip? Am I taking good care of my sobriety?

God grant that all of my empty places may be filled with God.

Slips don't just happen. We make room for them to happen.

Staying with the Program

"I will return to the house I left."—Matthew 12:44

While we may not consciously be aware of a desire to use, the "demon" is built into our disease. This desire is never completely dead. It is like an evil spirit, driven out, saying to itself, "I will return to the house I left." And, too often, it does just that, especially when we get away from our program—when we get too tired, hungry, and lonely.

When we least expect it.

When we stop our reading, meditation, prayer, attending meetings, and service.

Unless we put something creative and life-giving where once there were demons, we are placing ourselves in a very dangerous position.

Living one day at a time, letting go and letting God, and remembering that "easy does it" is always helpful for keeping our lives occupied with that which is good, positive, and life-giving.

Am I staying close to my program? Am I paying close attention to my spiritual growth?

God grant that I may stay close to my program each and every day.

Staying with the program is staying with sobriety.

May 2

AVOIDING OVERCONFIDENCE

> *"When [the evil spirit] arrives, it finds the house unoccupied, swept clean and put in order."*—MATTHEW 12:44

There is a danger called overconfidence, when we think we have done everything possible to avoid slips.

We may be doing many positive things to keep our sobriety and live it.

Everything is where it belongs, everything swept clean—everything in order.

But this also can be a very dangerous time, this overconfident time. It is at this time that we are very susceptible to a slip, just when we believe that we have a handle on sobriety, when we begin to think that we are too far along in our program to slip.

When such feelings begin to develop, it's important to pray for guidance, to have a talk with a sponsor, to share at meetings, to clear the decks of overconfidence and false pride.

Am I overconfident about my sobriety? Am I paying attention to my program?

God grant that I may not become overconfident about my sobriety.

It's not at all hard to have a slip, especially when we begin to think we never ever can.

BEING VIGILANT

"Then it goes and takes with it seven other spirits more wicked than itself, and they go in and live there. And the final condition is worse than the first."—MATTHEW 12:45

He had been sober twenty-five years. He had brought more people into the program than any other person. He had headed up a chemical treatment facility and was engaged in speaking engagements far and wide.

He was famous for his sobriety, helping thousands to sober up, and was also famous for his knowledge of the program

Then he was terminated, released from his high-profile position. He became intensely resentful, and he took a drink—then another and another and another.

In a short time he had to be hospitalized.

Unable to let go of his resentment, he died drunk.

Am I being vigilant about my sobriety? Am I taking my sobriety for granted?

God grant that I may always be vigilant.

Slips don't just happen. We set ourselves up for them.

May 4

DOING THE WILL OF GOD

> *"For whoever does the will of my Father in heaven is my brother and sister and mother."*—MATTHEW 12:50

We remember how it felt not to be doing the will of God. Who wants to go back to any of that, the deceit, the dishonesty with ourselves, others, and God? Trying to keep up with ourselves, always owing someone an explanation as to why we did things we should have left undone, or didn't do what we had promised to do.

We do know for certain that God wants us sober. It is God's will that we do not use.

In doing the will of God we become related to others and to God—connected in the fellowship of the Spirit.

Therefore, in the morning, we ask God to help us stay clean and sober "just for today"—one day at a time.

And before we go to sleep at night we give thanks for another day of sobriety.

These are the simple steps that help to keep us on the path, doing the will of God—staying sober.

Am I doing the will of God? Am I carefully watching over my sobriety?

God grant that I may stay clean and sober today.

Staying sober is God's will for us and our lives.

Being Receptive to God's Gifts

> *"A farmer went out to sow his seed. As he was scattering the seed, some fell along the path, and the birds came and ate it up."*—MATTHEW 13:3–4

Jesus tells the parable of a sower who went out to sow his field with new seed.

The seed was broadcast without holding back, falling in places where there could be growth and where growth would be impeded.

There have been times in our lives when the good news of promised recovery fell on deaf ears, even though deep in our hearts was hidden the hope of our salvation.

If we let down on the working of our program, forgetting the promises of the Lord to help and to heal, we are certain to be living on a hardened surface of life, vulnerable to being swallowed up.

Am I staying open to the Word of God? Am I receptive to God's gifts, which are offered to me day by day?

God grant that I may remain receptive and growing each day.

Being receptive to God's gifts is the doorway to sobriety.

May 6

TAKING GOOD CARE OF OURSELVES

"Some [seed] fell on rocky places, where it did not have much soil. It sprang up quickly, because the soil was shallow. But when the sun came up, the plants were scorched, and they withered because they had no root."—MATTHEW 13:5–6

There is also the danger of eagerly getting into our program for recovery, and then easing off, not going deeply enough into reading, prayer, meditation, attending meetings, serving others.

Then come times of testing that are like the scorching sun beating down on us. Because of spiritual neglect we can find ourselves without a sufficient root system, liable to shrivel and die.

If we are to stay spiritually alive and well, we must keep the roots of our recovery systems watered with the Word and promises of God.

Am I being watchful? Am I taking my program seriously and working it faithfully, taking good care of myself?

God grant that I may take good care of myself.

Taking good care of ourselves is our first responsibility—to ourselves.

AVOIDING DANGEROUS DIVERSIONS

> *"Other seed fell among thorns, which grew up and choked the plants."*—MATTHEW 13:7

Each of us must make specific decisions.
What am I going to do with myself?
With whom am I going to associate?
Can I keep all of my old friends?
Can I go to certain places?
A very real and constant danger, of course, is that of being overcome by circumstances beyond our control.

Many have fallen into thorn patches that have choked off their sobriety, leaving them stranded, isolated, alone.

Working the program keeps us focused on proven steps that prevent us from having our new life choked off by the many thorns of life.

Am I being careful with myself? Am I staying away from thorn patches that threaten to choke off my new life?

God grant that I may not be choked out of my sobriety.

There are some places that are absolutely deadly for us.

May 8

BEING OPEN AND RECEPTIVE TO GOD'S GIFTS

> *"Still other seed fell on good soil, where it produced a crop—a hundred, sixty or thirty times what was sown."*—MATTHEW 13:8

How did our lives take on a new focus, unhampered by any further need to use, to destroy ourselves?

Is it because we made a New Year's resolution, because we exercised a strong will to quit? Or were we simply ready to receive God's gifts of grace?

Can we even begin to say that we had become good soil for God to plant the seeds and have them nurtured? Yes, we can say that with humility and deeply felt gratitude.

One day, and very unexpectedly, we became the right kind of soil for God to plant a new garden of new life, new hope, and new joy.

And this is the miracle of grace.

Am I staying receptive to the gifts of God? Am I open to receive what God is ready to give?

God grant that I may always be receptive to gifts of grace.

When we let God do the planting, our lives bear beautiful fruit.

CELEBRATING THE MYSTERIES OF GOD

> *"The knowledge of the secrets of the kingdom of heaven has been given to you, but not to them."*
> —MATTHEW 13:11

The "secrets" about which Jesus is speaking are also called "mysteries".

These mysteries involve things we have discovered and known that many do not know and are unable to share with us.

For instance, the mystery of how one day we stopped using, just when it seemed absolutely impossible to do so.

There are other spiritual mysteries that keep us clean and sober in spite of turmoil and tension. We can't explain these mysteries either. But we can see them happening in ourselves and others who are recovering.

Am I aware of the mysteries of God at work in my life? Am I celebrating what God has done and is doing with me?

God grant me the capacity to believe the mysteries of recovery and celebrate them

Being involved with the mysteries of God is being involved in all that really matters.

May 10

INVESTING AND RECEIVING

> *"Whoever has will be given more, and he will have an abundance."*—MATTHEW 13:12

When we stay with our program for recovery, the blessings continue to grow, even when times are more difficult and testing more severe.

"I don't have to drink today." This is always the starting point. From there everything is better—better than when we were using.

When sober, we are able to take advantage of new opportunities to grow spiritually, to become more mature in our dealings with ourselves, with others, and with life—especially because we are letting go and letting God.

The more we invest ourselves in the program and process of recovery, the more faith, hope, and love we receive in return, because that is the eternal equation on which we can count.

Am I investing myself in my program for recovery? Am I receiving the benefits of new life, new hope, and new joy?

God grant that I may invest myself totally in my program for recovery.

When sober, we always receive more than we give.

Staying in There

> *"Whoever does not have, even what he has will be taken from him."*—MATTHEW 13:12

Today we have the other side of yesterday's equation.

When we don't invest ourselves in our program, negative things begin to happen. We begin to lose faith, hope, and the capacity to love, as the gains we had begin to slip away.

We don't attend to our reading, prayer, meditation.

We begin to slough off.

As our attitudes begin to deteriorate, our sobriety is threatened by neglect.

If we continue the pattern of noninvestment, we lose.

What we may have gained is taken away, and we alone are responsible for the relapse. No one else can be held accountable for our condition.

Actually we don't slip from sobriety, we give it away. So it's important to stay with our program.

Am I paying too little attention to my program of recovery? Am I letting go of the treasures I have received?

God grant that I may not lose what has been gained.

If we don't use it, we lose it.

May 12

HEARING—SEEING—BELIEVING

> *"Blessed are your eyes because they see, and your ears because they hear."*—MATTHEW 13:16

Remember how it used to be? The pain of confusion, anxiety, defeat? Not knowing what we were doing, where we had been, what we said, where we left the car? The blackouts? The contemplations of suicide?

Our sense of discouragement was deep.

Now, however, we are seeing and hearing new things that once seemed far from us, because of barriers we built within ourselves.

Now we are hearing and believing that we are human beings loved by God, hearing and believing that we can have self-worth because we are worth a lot to the Lord, experiencing changes in our life—more faith, hope, and love.

Am I aware of the work of the Lord in my life? Am I seeing and hearing the good news of recovery in myself and others?

God grant that I may see and hear the good news of recovery.

Seeing and hearing good news is vital for our recovery to continue.

WAITING FOR GOD TO WORK

> *"The kingdom of heaven is like yeast that a woman took and mixed into a large amount of flour until it worked all through the dough."*—MATTHEW 13:33

When we do the Steps they have a yeast-like effect that permeates our entire being.

We cannot rush this process.

Nor can we side-step, zigging and zagging our way through.

All of that is a waste of time and energy.

In order to become the new creatures that God wants us be, we have to think of ourselves as being infiltrated by the yeast-like Spirit of the Lord, allowing sufficient time for ourselves to become filled with a new faith, hope, and love—remembering that recovery is a process rather than a game of leapfrog.

There is not a single part of the process that we don't need or can do without, as we wait for God to move in our lives.

Am I seeing my recovery as a process? Am I waiting on the Lord to fill my spirit with God's Spirit?

God grant that I be filled with the yeast of the Spirit.

Patience—trusting God to work in us—is a virtue that we all need.

GOING AFTER THE BEST

> *"The kingdom of heaven is like treasure hidden in a field. When a man found it, he hid it again, and then in his joy went and sold all he had and bought that field."*—MATTHEW 13:44

Now that we have a taste of sobriety, isn't it like finding a real treasure that we want to keep at any and all costs?

Isn't it heartening going to meetings, hearing others report how they prize their sobriety and what God is doing in their lives? We hear so many stories of horrendous troubles that at one time would have shot any of us down.

But, praise the Lord, now it is different.

Now we know a new sense of peace and contentment, in spite of all obstacles.

Now there is nothing we will not do in order to keep what we have tasted: the fruits of the kingdom of heaven in a life of sobriety.

Am I keeping myself focused on the treasures of sobriety? Am I willing to do joyfully whatever is necessary to stay clean and sober today?

God grant that I may keep myself focused on the treasures of the kingdom of heaven.

Sobriety is worth every bit of what it costs.

HOLDING ON TO THE PEARL OF GREAT PRICE

> *"The kingdom of heaven is like a merchant looking for fine pearls. When he found one of great value, he went away and sold everything he had and bought it."*
> —MATTHEW 13:45–46

What won't we give to keep our sobriety? Why do we have such a high regard for our sobriety?

Isn't it because we remember what it was like not to be sober?

Isn't it because we remember the early morning sweating and fear, the near panic that engulfed us, and the inability to focus?

Have we not now, in a sense, sold all that we had in order to stay sober?

Are we not giving up our false pride, grandiosity, self-pity, resentments, and whatever else is needed for us to stay sober?

And isn't it true that we have come to see what a pearl of great price sobriety is? A treasure we wouldn't trade for anything, ever.

Do I prize my sobriety above anything else? Am I happy with the choice I have made to stay sober?

God grant that I may always prize my sobriety.

Sobriety is a pearl of great price.

May 16

Being Caught Up in Love

> *"The kingdom of heaven is like a net that was let down into the lake and caught all kinds of fish."*—MATTHEW 13:47

It is as though a great net has been cast out over the earth, and we are caught up in it by a power greater than ourselves.

And that power is God.

We did nothing to get into the net. As a matter of fact, most of us did everything possible to avoid the net of love, to stay where we were in the black depths of the sea.

But then it happened: We became encircled by love and hauled up into the boat where the Lord began to sort us out, each to our own place.

Some are thrown back into the sea because it's not their time to be possessed by love.

But thank God for the net. Thank God for having caught us up.

Am I satisfied with my situation? Am I glad to have been caught up in the net of God's love?

God grant that I may be caught up in the net of divine love, each and every day.

Being caught in God's net of love is to be caught up in an eternity of light.

COMING INTO UNDERSTANDING

> *"Have you understood all these things?"*—MATTHEW 13:51

Wasn't it part of our self-imposed "duty" to know everything there is to know, to have strong opinions, and a lot of stubbornness, which we considered a virtue backed up by self-will? Also backed up by an abundance of self-centered opinions.

Jesus isn't looking for our opinions when he asks, "Have you understood all these things?"

Do we understand that we are sober because God's grace finally has pierced the barriers of pride and self-sufficiency?

Do we understand that it is only by the grace of God that any of us are sober today—rather than by our willpower?

Do I understand what has happened to me? Do I understand what is happening to me now?

God grant that I may understand the true foundations for my sobriety.

Understanding what is happening to us is an important key to a healthy, long-lasting, and growing sobriety.

May 18

REMEMBERING THE COMPASSION OF THE LORD

> *When Jesus landed and saw a large crowd, he had compassion on them and healed their sick.*—MAT-THEW 14:14

How many of us are there? Millions! All over the face of the earth—throngs of men and women like ourselves, whose lives have been turned into turmoil and desolation because of alcohol and other drugs.

And we who are recovering from this dreaded disease know the meaning of compassion.

Have we not experienced the compassion of the Lord working in our lives, picking us up when we were hopelessly down and out, when our lives were out of control, when we needed to be restored to sanity because we could not come back on our own?

Now, where once there only were two and three and ten and twelve, the healing ones number in the millions.

Am I grateful for Christ's compassion working in my life? Am I sharing that compassion with others?

God grant that I may be eternally grateful for the compassion of the Lord given to me.

Remembering the compassion by which we got sober is very important for our continued sobriety.

BEING SATISFIED

They all ate and were satisfied.—MATTHEW 14:20

Of course we do not always feel satisfied with our lives, the way things are going for us or the world. But this is true for almost everyone.

On the other hand, we experience more satisfaction in our sobriety, a deeper kind of satisfaction than we have known before. We know where we would be had we not entered sobriety.

We have also learned that the Lord feeds anyone who wants to be fed, that we only have to be willing and open to the grace of God coming into our lives.

And if we have ever treated ourselves to large gatherings of recovering brothers and sisters, we know about the joy of being satisfied.

At such times we experience a sense of deep satisfaction that cannot be surpassed—deep, heartfelt gratitude for the gifts of God so abundantly given to such as we.

Now we, who once were starving, are being fed; we who once knew no satisfaction are being satisfied.

Am I finding satisfaction in my sobriety? Am I grateful for the gifts of God given to me?

God grant that I may always find satisfaction in my sobriety.

Finding satisfaction is possible when we are sober.

May 20

AFFIRMING OUR DOUBT

> *"You of little faith, why did you doubt?"*—MATTHEW
> 14:31

There are times of doubt for all of us, because we
are human beings.

Not always are we on top of our game. Not always
do we believe God or believe in ourselves.

Not always do we feel like staying sober. Sometimes we get thirsty and begin to doubt that we are
going to stay sober.

As trials and tribulations arise, we may doubt our
capacity to weather the storms.

Some days it feels as though we could walk on
water, while other days we feel as if we will surely
sink if we try.

What's important is that we are still on the path.

Doubting and sinking is all part of this process.

But another part of the process is to be caught by
the Lord and lifted up, day after day.

Am I doubting the power of God? Am I spiritually
slipping and sliding?

God grant that I remain faithful.

Doubting isn't the problem. Denial is the problem.

TRUSTING THOSE WHO KNOW

"If a blind man leads a blind man, both will fall into a pit."—MATTHEW 15:14

In recovery we are always in need of guidance, day by day—even moment by moment; because we still have some of our night blindness.

It is still difficult to discern, to choose what is best for ourselves. We need someone to lead us: a guide, a sponsor.

We need a friend who can see for us—our Lord and the Spirit.

We must avoid the counsel of those who, like ourselves, cannot clearly see the way we are to be going.

Obviously, we mustn't depend on someone who is still using.

Our most dependable guide is Christ.

Christ is not blind to our needs.

Christ not only knows the way, he is the Way.

Christ is our eyes and ears—our friend and guide.

Am I trusting someone who knows the way? Am I trusting Christ to lead me?

God grant that I may be led where I am to be going.

Staying sober is being led by someone who knows the way.

HAVING FAITH AND DESIRE

> *"Woman, you have great faith! Your request is granted."*—MATTHEW 15:28

Our program has to do with faith.

By faith we turn to God to help us.

By faith we attend our meetings, believing that we can strengthen one another, and build a better life for ourselves as a fellowship.

By faith we read our literature, pray, meditate, and enter into service.

By faith we approach each day with a prayer of asking: "God keep me clean and sober today."

By faith we offer our thanksgiving to the Lord before going to sleep: "Thank you Lord for giving me this day of sobriety."

By faith we believe that God can do for us what we cannot do for ourselves.

How is my desire to stay clean and sober today? Do I have faith that God can do for me what I cannot do for myself?

God grant me the faith and desire to stay sober today.

Faith in God and the desire to stay sober is the combination that never fails.

GIVING GLORY TO GOD

> *"And they praised the God of Israel."*—MATTHEW
> 15:31

Giving credit where credit is due is fundamental
for our recovery.

The ego wants to take the credit, to accept the
praise.

However, from our own experience and the collective experience of our fellowship, we know that to
take credit for our sobriety is to enter dangerous
territory where grandiosity takes over, divesting us of
needed acceptance and surrender to stay sober.

People watched as Jesus healed, and they glorified
God. We watch as others become sober and give
glory to God.

Ours is a spiritual program.

Each day is a new beginning of glorifying God
through unity, recovery, and service.

Am I giving glory to God for my sobriety? Am I
sharing the goodness of God with others?

*God grant that I may always remember that my help
comes from the Lord.*

Giving glory to God will never get us into needless
trouble.

REMEMBERING THE PROMISES

"I will give you the keys of the kingdom of heaven."
—MATTHEW 16:19

Inasmuch as we stay with our program for recovery we are given promises, promises that come from a long time ago; promises placed in language we understand, long for, and desire. They are the keys to the kingdom.

We are going to know a new freedom and a new happiness.

We will not regret the past, nor wish to shut the door on it.

We will comprehend the word serenity, and we will know peace.

No matter how far down the scale we have gone, we will see how our experience can benefit others.

Am I remembering the promises of God? Am I working my program so as to experience the promises?

God grant me the promised keys to the kingdom.

Some promises mean more than other promises.

BINDING AND LOOSENING

> *"Whatever you bind on earth will be bound in heaven,*
> *and whatever you loose on earth will be loosed in*
> *heaven."*—MATTHEW 16:19

Whatever we choose to do with our lives has meaning and sticking power.

When we build trust, we are trusted. When we manipulate, exploit, and otherwise use people, we build distrust.

If we decide to trust God, to stay sober, to be honest and upright in all of our transactions, we are tied into goodness and mercy, into positive life-giving energy that follows us into eternity.

By the same token, if we choose to be bound by negative energy, the results are going to be negative.

Nothing is ever lost. Everything that happens is inscribed on our conscious or unconscious self.

There are consequences for whatever we choose to do with our lives—both positive and negative.

Am I binding myself to that which is good? Am I doing what is best for me?

God grant that I may be bound up by that which is good and life-giving.

What we decide to do with ourselves is very important business.

May 26

LETTING GO

> *"Whoever wants to save his life will lose it, and who-
> ever loses his life for me will find it."*—MATTHEW
> 16:25

We are told that if we think only of ourselves,
without giving, we will surely fail.

In this program not only is it wise and prudent to
give, it is a life-giving necessity.

To keep our sobriety, we must share it with others—giving it away by telling our story, by helping
others, by working Step Twelve of the program, by
putting down the demands of the ego, by losing in
order to find.

Having had a spiritual awakening as the result of
these steps, we carry the message to others who still
are suffering. We lose ourselves in the doing of this
for healthy-selfish reasons. By losing our lives in this
manner, we find life. Just as Jesus promises.

Am I sharing the joys of my recovery with others?
Am I carrying the message?

God grant that I may give up my life to find it.

If we never let go, we never get there.

GAINING, NOT LOSING

"What good will it be for a man, if he gains the whole world, yet forfeits his soul?"—MATTHEW 16:26

We can remember the earlier days of our using— the warm jolt in the stomach that spread over our bodies—that made us feel everything was going to be all right in the world and all right for us.

It was as though we had gained the whole world as the tension disappeared, as the pain went away, as we felt in control of our lives, even though everything was out of control.

To maintain our "hold" we had to lie to ourselves, to others, to God.

We were out of control, pretending to be in control.

We were losers pretending to be winners.

And there was only one hope for us, if we were not literally to lose our lives. That hope had to begin with abstinence.

Am I keeping my attention focused on staying sober today? Am I investing my life where it will do me the most good?

God grant that I may have new life, new hope, and new joy.

It's what we put into life that counts.

CHOOSING LIFE

> *"What can a man give in exchange for his soul?"*
> —MATTHEW 16:26

Millions are choosing death by bottle, pill, nicotine, whatever the drug is. And that's the answer to our scripture's question for today.

Nevertheless, in all of us there is a longing for new life, hidden as that longing may be.

It was life we were seeking in bottles and pills. But not all of us are ready to take the necessary steps of acceptance and surrender that provide access to life.

Becoming willing is the first step into new life, new hope, and new joy—through a lasting, healthy, ever-growing sobriety.

The answer to the scripture's question, is that we are willing to let God do whatever is required for us to have a healthy life of sobriety.

Am I willing to stay sober, regardless of the cost? Am I ready to let God do for me what I cannot do for myself?

God grant me the gifts of acceptance and surrender.

Each day brings the question, "What are you ready and willing to do for your life today?"

MOVING MOUNTAINS OF OBSTRUCTION

> *"I tell you the truth, if you have faith as small as a mustard seed, you can say to this mountain, 'Move from here to there' and it will move."*—MATTHEW 17:20

Sobriety is based on possibilities. The possibility that God can do for us what we cannot do for ourselves. The possibility that we can refrain from using, one day at a time. The possibility that by keeping our lives as simple as possible we will stay sober.

For us this is the moving of immovable mountains.

For us this is tunneling through impassable places, crossing uncrossable ridges.

For us all things are possible because God specializes in things thought impossible, doing for us what no other power can do.

Do I have faith in the power of God and my program for recovery? Am I putting my faith to work in all the details of my life?

God grant me the faith that moves mountains of fear.

Nothing is impossible—not for God.

BEING LIKE A CHILD

"Unless you change and become like little children, you will never enter the kingdom of heaven."—MATTHEW 18:3

A sponsor said to someone he was trying to help: "You go to meetings, see? And you listen to what they say. You hear me? You won't understand what they are talking about—not right away. But I want you to listen, and don't argue with them. Understand? Do what they tell you, like you're a little child eager to learn, and everything will turn out OK. See?"

This makes us feel like little children.

But if we listen and trust and do what we are told, pretty soon we begin to see.

Until we set aside our false pride and become as little children, we very likely will not stay sober.

Trusting, as only a child is able to trust.

Am I humbly accepting the wisdom and leading of others? Am I trusting the power of God to heal?

God grant that I may be open to what is offered.

Sobriety is easier once we have broken the barrier of false pride.

BEING HUMBLY GRATEFUL

"Whoever humbles himself like this child is the greatest in the kingdom of heaven."—MATTHEW 18:4

Maintaining a healthy and growing sobriety has everything to do with attitude.

When the attitude is negative, sobriety is not healthy.

But as we said yesterday, if and when we are ready to enter the program of recovery with the expectation and excitement of a child—without trying to direct the traffic—we enter a new life of happy sobriety, little by little, one day at a time.

Humble people are sober people.

Contentedly sober.

Happily sober.

Without regrets—sober.

Without fear, anger, and resentment—sober.

By being the least, by being the servants, we become the greatest in innocence and blessedness.

Humbly and gratefully—sober.

Am I being humble and grateful for my sobriety? Am I being the servant of others?

God grant that I may be humbly grateful for my sobriety.

Grandiosity is a certain step—over a cliff.

June 1

DOING RADICAL SURGERY

> *"If your hand or your foot causes you to sin, cut it off and throw it away."*—MATTHEW 18:8

A most amazing saying states simply: "If we don't drink, we won't get drunk." So throw away the bottle.

A simple and ancient spiritual teaching says: Get rid of everything that doesn't work, that gets in the way, that leads us into places where we can hurt ourselves.

There are things we simply must get rid of if we are to stay sober. Amputation is the first step in our recovery.

We have to cut away from the bottle, the pills, the excessive food. Over and out.

Sobriety calls for radical surgery. We're not going to like it, but that's not the issue.

Am I willing to let go of all that can do me harm? Am I ready to protect my sobriety at all costs?

God grant that I may let go of everything that is harmful to me.

Doing what is painless doesn't always alleviate our pain.

ACCEPTING OUR VALUE TO GOD

> *"What do you think? If a man owns a hundred sheep, and one of them wanders away, will he not leave the ninety-nine on the hills and go to look for the one that wandered off?"*—MATTHEW 18:12

We know what it is to go astray, to be lost.

If there is any feeling that makes us sad, it's that sensation of being lost. We remember being in places where we felt alone, where it seemed no one could possibly be with us.

All the time, Christ was with us. But we couldn't sense his presence.

Now, however, it is becoming ever more clear that someone came looking for us because we were worth something—even a "precious" something.

We are loved and sought after by God—lifted, carried, and restored.

Isn't it time that we accept our value to God?

Am I aware of my value to God? Am I accepting my value to God?

God grant that I may be grateful for Christ, the Good Shepherd of my soul.

You can't be too lost to get found.

June 3

FOCUSING ON FORGIVENESS

> *"Lord, how many times shall I forgive my brother
> when he sins against me? Up to seven times?"*—MAT-
> THEW 18:21

Seven times, the law of forgiveness says—seven
times forgive someone who offends you. Then that's
enough.

Where do we draw the line?

When do we say, "This is enough!"

And what about our offenses against God?

Are seven offenses enough?

Or should we be allowed "up to" seven offenses,
or maybe not that many? Maybe two or four or three
or one?

It's not that we should ever play patsy for someone
who chooses to run roughshod over us. That's not
the meaning of forgiveness.

But when is enough enough?

Who is to decide?

And how?

Am I ready to forgive? Am I ready to continue forgiving?

God grant that I may forgive as I am being forgiven.

Pretending forgiveness is dangerous to our sobriety

LETTING GO OF RESENTMENT

"I tell you, not seven times, but seventy-seven times."
—MATTHEW 18:22

So we must let go of malice, not periodically, but right along—as a way of life.

Sometimes this is easier said than done.

In our program we are reminded: "Resentment is the *number one* offender. It destroys more alcoholics than anything else. From it stem all forms of spiritual disease, for we have been not only mentally and physically ill, we have been spiritually sick."

Certainly this applies to all people, but for those of us who are trying to recover, there can be no limits to our letting go and letting God settle the accounts—as God sees them.

We are not being asked to let others walk all over us. But we are being asked to let go of resentment that is capable of destroying us completely.

Am I carrying any resentments? Am I trying to get back at anyone?

God grant that I harbor no grudges and carry no resentments.

Carried resentments can break the back of sobriety.

June 5

ACCEPTING WHAT IS OFFERED

> *"Not everyone can accept this teaching, but only those to whom it has been given."*—MATTHEW 19:11

What is a good recovery like?

It's like going to your exercise program every day, eager and ambitious; totally invested in the accepted rigors that keep the body toned and healthy.

Says one very happy exerciser: "I look forward to this exercise every day. It makes me happy. I feel good. I feel sorry for people who haven't learned how to enjoy it."

So it is with maintaining a good sobriety.

We begin to sense there is something special about us, that we have received gifts that others seem to have missed.

Gifts of willingness to let go and let God, willingness to forgive and forget, together with an eager readiness to serve.

Am I accepting and receiving what God offers? Am I staying sober with gratitude and joyful living?

God grant that I may gratefully accept what is being offered for my salvation.

New life belongs to those who are ready to receive God's gifts with gratitude and joy.

GOING ALL THE WAY

> *"If you want to be perfect, go, sell your possessions and give to the poor, and you will have treasure in heaven. Then come, follow me."*—MATTHEW 19:21

We must have real commitment if we want to go on with a healthy sobriety.

Commitment means requirements, demands, opportunities, and privileges.

Requirements: that we want a new life more than anything else—more than possessions, honor, riches, popularity, acceptability.

Demands: that we are ready to do battle with our egos, with the need to be first, the best, the ultimate.

Opportunities: the chance to save our lives, to live abundantly.

Privileges: the opportunity to share our sobriety with others and to grow spiritually.

Am I willing to make the leap? Am I ready to build my sobriety and keep it?

God grant that I may go all the way into a healthy sobriety, doing whatever is called for to make this possible.

There is only one workable way, and that's all the way.

June 7

PUTTING FIRST THINGS FIRST

> *"I tell you the truth, it is hard for a rich man to enter the kingdom of heaven."*—MATTHEW 19:23

When something gets in the path of our sobriety and obstructs it, recovery becomes very difficult.

It's like the rich young man who wanted to come to Jesus while maintaining allegiance to his first loyalty—money.

He could see Jesus only through the fog of his wealth, which meant that he couldn't let go and freely relate his life to the Lord.

This left him feeling bad: "He went away sad, because he had great wealth."

In the program we always are saying simple-sounding things: "Easy does it"—"Let go, let God"—"One day at a time"—"Keep it simple"—"Turn it over"—"First things first."

Whatever gets in the way of our sobriety must be set aside, perhaps with sorrow, but without regrets.

Am I having conflicts of interest? Am I putting first things first?

God grant that I may put first things first.

Sobriety is going after it, full steam ahead.

STAYING HAPPILY SOBER

> *"Again I tell you, it is easier for a camel to go through the eye of a needle than for a rich man to enter the kingdom of God."*—MATTHEW 19:24

Whatever comes between ourselves and God makes it very difficult, if not impossible, to maintain a happy, sober life.

As a basic part of our recovery program we must learn how to face facts about the nature of recovery into rebirth.

Fact: It's impossible to stay *happily sober* if we don't want to stay sober.

Fact: It's impossible to stay *happily sober* if we let anything or anyone get in the way of our program, including the making of money.

There are some things that have to be done if we want to maintain a healthy sobriety. The first is to clear the decks and put first things first.

Am I serving God first, and above all? Am I happily sober?

God grant that I may let nothing get in the way of my sobriety.

Being happily sober is the object of recovery and its reward.

June 9

Waiting Our Turn

> "When evening came, the owner of the vineyard said to his foreman, 'Call the workers and pay them their wages, beginning with the last ones hired and going on to the first.'" —MATTHEW 20:8

We can remember how it felt. Other people getting ahead of us because of "good luck":

Because we weren't appreciated for all we did and had to offer.

Even though we claimed to be doing our best, others got more of the pie than we did, and got it first. Recognition, raises, favors, honor, glory.

Sometimes those who came after us were given preferential treatment, which really made us feel bad and created a lot of resentment.

Now, however, our perspective is changing.

We are beginning to realize that there are times for everyone when life seems unfair. We also are learning to wait our turn.

Waiting our turn is helping us grow.

Am I waiting my turn? Am I content?

God grant that I may wait my turn without resentment.

Waiting our turn is essential to the growth process.

BEING LAST AND FIRST

"So the last will be first, and the first will be last."
—MATTHEW 20:16

There's a strange equation in the recovery process, in our spiritual growth and development, that has to do with priorities.

In the world of finance, for instance, to have the most money is to be first. In sports, to win is to be first. The strongest get their way, the weak have to wait. And pretty people get preferential treatment.

In our using days it often was just like that. People didn't want us around. We were burdensome. We were being left behind, even as we struggled so hard to be somewhere near the head of the line.

Now we are on a different course, no longer struggling to be first—only to be sober and straight, honest and dependable—which is the best of all.

Am I doing what is right for me? Am I taking one step at a time?

God grant that I may be sober, straight, honest, and dependable.

Being first in our own hearts is the "first" that really counts.

June 11

BEING A SERVANT

> *"Whoever wants to become great among you must be your servant."*—MATTHEW 20:26

Even though servanthood is a beautiful concept, not all of us respond to it quickly or resolutely.

However, we do feel warmly toward trusted and unselfish servants, agreeing that if everyone were that way the world would be a much better place.

Servants do all sorts of work—scrubbing floors, growing food, picking up the garbage, writing, designing, digging ditches, building houses, baking bread, doing brain surgery.

In our program we know that shared giving is servanthood, and that servanthood keeps us sober. Thus there can be no conflict between us as long as no one is trying to be above anyone else.

We are trying to help one another stay sober, and others to become sober. This requires the kind of giving that can be done only by a servant.

Am I becoming the servant? Am I helping myself by serving others?

God grant that I may be a servant of Christ by serving others.

Being a servant is being alive and well.

BECOMING READY AND OPEN

> *"What do you think? There was a man who had two
> sons. He went to the first and said, 'Son, go and work
> today in the vineyard.' He said, 'I will not,' but later
> he changed his mind and went."*—MATTHEW 21:-
> 28–29

Actually, we still don't know why someone
changes.

We know that our kind of change can't be
learned, simply because we didn't think ourselves
into a new frame of mind.

Something new just popped one day, and we came
up with a different perspective, with new receptivity
to change. It awed us, and awed others as well.

Now we have gone to work in God's vineyard as
servants.

Now we are cooperating with others, and our stubborn streak is softening.

Am I more open and ready to do the work of the
servant? Am I becoming less stubborn?

*God grant that I may willingly do what is necessary
and right.*

Becoming open and ready is exciting and rewarding.

KEEPING OUR WORD

> *"Then the father went to the other son and said the same thing. He answered, 'I will, sir,' but he did not go."*—MATTHEW 21:30

"I'm going to do it. I'm going to change. I'll take care of it." Words, words, words, and more words.

More promises. More broken promises. Broken promises to ourselves, to others, and to God.

It wasn't that we didn't think we were honest, or weren't trying to be honest. It was just that we couldn't be truthful, to stand behind our words, to do what we said we were going to do.

And people lost trust, didn't believe us anymore, even though they wanted to.

We didn't know how to commit ourselves to a new way of life.

But now things are beginning to change, although everything worthwhile takes time.

Now we are learning to do what we say.

Am I keeping my word? Am I doing what I say I will do?

God grant that I may do what I promise to do.

Keeping our word is keeping the best we have to offer.

LOVING GOD

> " 'Love the Lord your God with all your heart and with
> all your soul and with all your mind.' This is the first
> and greatest commandment."—MATTHEW 22:37–38

Our program begins and ends with God: God's presence, God's promises, God's grace, God's ever-present help to keep us sober and growing, one day at a time.

When we begin loving God, interesting and exciting things happen to us—such as a dwindling of self-centeredness and self-will, coupled with the capacity to trust, to love, and to serve.

Loving God with all our heart and soul and mind is offering all we have for the welfare of the earth and its people.

Loving God is to express gratitude for all blessings received, undeserved as they are.

As the song says, "Reach out and touch somebody." That is loving God.

Am I loving God with all of my heart, mind, and soul? Am I serving God day by day?

God grant me a heart filled with love.

To love God is to come alive. To serve God is to be alive.

June 15

LOVING AND SHARING

> *And the second [greatest commandment] is like it:
> 'Love your neighbor as yourself.' "*—MATTHEW 22:39

Sobriety isn't gained or maintained in isolation, but in relation, in loving and serving relationships with others.

As we relate to one another through acts of caring and sharing our commonalty, our frailty—our need for God and one another—the bonds of love and fellowship grow stronger.

By sharing ourselves, one with another, we discover our commonality to be the basic support system.

We are called into the fellowship of recovering people, where relationship is bonded by the sharing of experience, both the joy of victory and the agony of defeat. Most of all, we share the hope that is in us for recovery and newness of life.

Am I learning to love myself? Am I learning to share myself with others?

God grant that I may love myself, and my neighbor as myself.

Sharing is loving. Loving is sharing.

ACCEPTING RESPONSIBILITY FOR OURSELVES

> *"[The kingdom of heaven] is like a man going on a journey, who called his servants and entrusted his property to them."*—MATTHEW 25:14

For many of us there are the three legacies of AA—recovery, unity, and service—passed down and entrusted to each new generation.

How we receive these gifts and what we choose to do with them is vital for our sobriety and spiritual health, our growth and development.

Accepting both the gifts and responsibility for them is the lifeblood of recovery, in the best sense of the word.

Once we enter into the three legacies of unity, recovery, and service, we begin to experience what it means to be true and vital human beings.

Am I accepting responsibility for what has been entrusted to me? Am I grateful for the gifts bestowed on me?

God grant that I may accept personal responsibility for all gifts given to me.

Taking good care of what has been given is the great privilege of recovery.

June 17

ACCEPTING WHAT IS ENTRUSTED TO US TO DO

> *"To one he gave five talents of money, to another two talents, and to another one talent, each according to his ability."*—MATTHEW 25:14–15

To everyone in the program something has been entrusted, something specific, a talent or talents.

All of us have been entrusted with the commission to help one another recover and live.

Affirming our Lord's commission and accepting personal responsibility for it is the foundation stone of our continued sobriety, together with the life of the fellowship.

Each of us has been or will be given our own special responsibility to be invested, transmitted, and enlarged.

Unimportant as the responsibility may seem to be, it is meant to be worked and developed to its fullest possible potential, both for our personal benefit and the general welfare of all we are called to serve.

Am I accepting God's entrustments? Am I investing myself in what has been given to me to do?

God grant that I may invest myself in what I am being entrusted to do.

Entrustment is the key to recovery.

INVESTING OURSELVES

> *"The man who had received the five talents went at once and put his money to work and gained five more. So also, the one with the two talents gained two more."*
> —MATTHEW 25:16–17

By investing ourselves fully, we are able to add strength to the fellowship, helping ourselves and others to grow in faith, hope, and love.

At the close of each day it is important to ask, "What have I done today to increase the entrustment made to me? Have I been of help to someone, through the offering of prayers in their behalf, by a telephone call, by speaking at a meeting?"

Making this kind of inventory, each and every day, will keep our sobriety tuned up and add treasures to our spiritual growth.

Am I increasing the entrustments given to me? Am I sharing God's recovery gifts of faith, hope, and love with others?

God grant that I may increase the entrustments given to me.

The entrustment of sobriety always calls for the reinvestment of ourselves.

June 19

HIDING GOD'S ENTRUSTMENT

> *"But the man who had received the one talent went off, dug a hole in the ground and hid his master's money."*—MATTHEW 25:18

The man said to the master, "I know that you demand much of what you entrust, and I was afraid of losing the investment, so I hid it in the ground."

He pleaded caution, care, responsibility, but he missed the point completely. His entrustment was to reinvest, to increase the blessings.

The founders of AA knew the necessity of reinvestment for the sake of their own sobriety, knew that unless they reinvested themselves in the recovery and welfare of other suffering people they themselves would lose the gift of sobriety that had been given them.

Only by offering help to others were they able to keep their sobriety, to grow spiritually.

If we don't work with the entrustment of sobriety, we lose it.

Am I hiding the entrustment given to me? Am I burying the treasure of recovery given to me?

God grant that I may not hide the entrustment given to me.

Hiding God's entrustments can be fatal.

SETTLING ACCOUNTS

> *"After a long time the master of those servants returned and settled accounts with them."*—MATTHEW 25:19

We search out our character defects and confess them, making amends to those we have harmed.

We settle accounts with ourselves, with others, and with God.

Before sobering up we closed our eyes to settlement clauses in many of our agreed contracts with ourselves, with others, with God.

Now the settling of accounts need not be feared, not as long as we have made a decision to change and are in the process of changing—making restitution where possible.

Then the settlement cannot help but be in our favor, as we face both the positive and negative aspects of our personhood openly and honestly.

Am I settling all unsettled accounts? Am I making amends and restitution where necessary?

God grant that I may responsibly settle all unsettled accounts.

Settling accounts is the stepping-stone to a healthy and happy sobriety.

June 21

BEING AWARE OF GAIN

> *"The man who had received the five talents brought the other five. 'Master,' he said 'you entrusted me with five talents. See, I have gained five more.'"* —MATTHEW 25:20

This is why there is so much gratitude expressed by so many grateful recovering persons.

We sense that we have been entrusted with gifts we never could have imagined possible: faith, hope, and love, in recovery, unity, and service; self-respect and the respect of others; a growing conscious contact with God, with ourselves, with others.

The more we invest ourselves in the recovery process, the more we grow spiritually, and the greater are the rewards of sobriety: peace, joy, serenity, and growing capacity to deal with the contingencies of life.

Am I aware of the gains I am receiving from working my program? Am I grateful for the progress?

God grant that I may see and celebrate the gains I have made in the working of my program.

Looking back shows us how much we have been blessed and how far we have come.

BEING FAITHFUL

> *"Well done, good and faithful servant! You have been faithful with a few things; I will put you in charge of many things."*—MATTHEW 25:21

We do what is given us to be done.

"Whatever it is that God has given me to do, I intend to do all of it," is the attitude.

We are put in charge of certain responsibilities, but not "in charge" as a manipulator.

Being in charge doesn't mean being boss, doesn't mean telling others what to do with their lives, doesn't mean giving advice when advice isn't sought, doesn't mean being traffic directors.

We are entrusted with three beautiful legacies, as stated in AA: recovery, unity, and service. This charge is entrusted to us as we are making progress in our recovery, in the working of our program.

Am I being faithful to myself, to God, to the working of my program? Am I experiencing the promised gains of working the program?

God grant that I may be faithful to my calling to serve.

Being faithful to our calling is the energy of our sobriety.

June 23

Making Use of What Has Been Given

"The man with the two talents also came. 'Master,' he said, 'you entrusted me with two talents; see, I have gained two more.'"—MATTHEW 25:22

We come to acknowledge that some of us are given fewer gifts and lesser responsibilities than others, but the principle of investment remains intact, even if we have received relatively little in comparison to what others have received.

But that isn't the point.

Remember that the Lord is able to use the little bit we may have to invest.

Remember that it is our task to invest and reinvest the endowments God has provided to strengthen our legacies of recovery, unity, and service.

By giving of the little we have to offer we gain a great deal in faith, hope, love, joy, and serenity.

Am I investing all of the gifts given to me, no matter how few or how small they may be? Am I taking seriously this work of the Lord, helping other people to live?

God grant that I may use every talent given to me, to its very best advantage.

It's what we do with what we have received that counts up.

BEING READY TO INVEST

"I was afraid and went out and hid your talent in the ground. See, here is what belongs to you."—MATTHEW 25:25

Some of us seem to do little more than attend meetings and take what is offered. We put little or nothing back, and we sometimes utter excuses.

Often the excuse is that we are afraid: afraid that we are unable to do the work set before us, like giving a meeting at a detox center, or making any kind of a twelfth-Step call.

What we are forgetting, of course, is that we aren't the ones who are doing the work in the first place.

Rather, we are the "earthen vessels" called by our Lord to go into all the world with holy gifts and offer them to others in need.

Am I afraid to invest the gifts given to me? Am I worried about being insufficient, about failing?

God grant that I may take what I have been given and use it purposefully.

Being afraid of a given task is all right as long as we do what we are given to do.

June 25

ADDING ON

> *"Take the talent from him and give it to the one who has the ten talents."*—MATTHEW 5:28

Some people get more out of their lives than others. Why is this?

The answer is simple: Some people invest more of themselves into life than others.

Joyful sobriety comes from a complete investment of ourselves—physical, mental, spiritual.

When we don't invest ourselves, we are the losers. When we invest, we are the winners.

It's as simple as that.

There's an abundance that comes with good sobriety—not necessarily material, but always spiritual and emotional. The abundance of special gifts includes patience, the capacity for joy and gratitude, the ability to handle situations that once baffled us, and much more.

A new happiness.

Am I investing myself in recovery? Am I holding anything back?

God grant that I may not bury the gifts given to me.

Holding back on what has been given is life-threatening. Investing is life-giving.

CLAIMING WHAT IS OURS

> *"Come, you who are blessed by my Father; take your inheritance, the kingdom prepared for you since the creation of the world."*—MATTHEW 25:34

Sobriety is enhanced and strengthened once we see and understand that we are linked to the eternal from the very beginning.

When we become sober, we begin to inherit what we actually are, as part and parcel of God.

When we become sober, we begin to come into conscious contact with God, the source of our being. It is this contact that keeps us growing spiritually in our program.

When we become sober, we begin to inherit the goodness of God's kingdom of faith, hope, and love, rather than the horrors of self-will running riot.

Am I getting the most out of life by faithfully working my program? Am I claiming my inheritance of serenity, joy, and peace?

God grant me the inheritance of serenity, joy, and peace.

Claiming what is ours to have is claiming the kingdom of God.

June 27

REACHING OUT TO HELP

> *"For I was hungry and you gave me something to eat, I was thirsty and you gave me something to drink, I was a stranger and you invited me in."*—MATTHEW 25:35

Yesterday we talked about inheriting the kingdom of God, and today we are given the condition of such an inheritance.

The kingdom is ours when we do the will and the work of God in the world.

Remembering how we were accepted, how we were taken into the program for recovery, we know how it feels to be a stranger, how it feels to be welcomed in.

We know what it is like to be spiritually hungry, but also what it is to be fed the hope and promises of God.

When we give what has been given to us we are blessed. When we feed as we have been fed, and visit as we have been visited, our spiritual thirst is relieved.

Am I ministering to others? Am I reaching out to help?

God grant that I may reach out to help others.

Reaching out to others is helping ourselves to recover and to heal.

Helping as We Are Being Helped

"I needed clothes and you clothed me, I was sick and you looked after me, I was in prison and you came to visit me."—MATTHEW 25:36

Some of us go to prisons to minister, some offer other services to the needy, doing the best we can to carry the message of recovery, sharing what it was like for us, and what it is like now, offering our support.

Through service we experience the deepest blessings of our program.

Without service there is no program.

How can we ever forget that we were visited when our spirits were famished, when we were spiritually naked, when we were imprisoned by our disease?

Was it not because others reached out to us that we were given the privilege to reach out to others, as an offering of gratitude?

Am I offering myself to others? Am I gratefully sharing what has been given to me?

God grant that I may be of help where help is needed.

We must receive in order to give—and give in order to receive.

June 29

SEEING CHRIST IN OTHERS

"Then the righteous will answer him, 'Lord when did we see you hungry and feed you?'"—MATTHEW 25:- 38–39

True servants are quite unaware of their servant-hood, even while they are doing it.

Once in a while one may hear a burst of false pride at a meeting: "I did this or that."

But more often they are astounded when someone finds out and makes mention of the good works.

What's exciting is the universal attraction to service. For when we are serving another human being, we are serving the universal Christ, because Christ is somewhere in everyone, because Christ is of creation itself, and so are we.

Someone has said, "Look for the Christ in others, and let the Christ in you serve the Christ in them."

This is an excellent and most hopeful way to approach our service, realizing that when we serve someone else we are serving our Lord.

Am I seeing the Christ in others? Am I ministering to those whom Christ brings me to serve?

God grant that I may minister to the Christ in others.

Ministering to others is ministering to Christ.

MAKING NO DISTINCTIONS

> *"I tell you the the truth, whatever you did for one of the least of these brothers of mine, you did for me."*
> —MATTHEW 25:40

We dare not be choosey when we are called upon to help others who suffer.

Sometimes this is difficult to accept.

For instance, there is nothing happy about dealing with falling-down drunks.

Nevertheless we pray to become willing servants; willing to minister to anyone Christ sets before us, at the appropriate time.

In our ministry there is no distinction because of race, creed, color, or economic or social status.

Once we have settled into this frame of mind—this attitude of acceptance—doors begin to open for service we never could have expected, and blessings begin to abound.

Am I being choosey about the people I seek to serve? Am I willing to minister to anyone Christ sets before me?

God grant that I may be open to minister to all who are set before me.

Being choosey about whom we serve is not part of our calling.

July 1

PRAYING FOR GOD'S WILL TO BE DONE

"Not as I will, but as you will."—MATTHEW 26:39

God's will is for a whole new way of life: a life of acceptance and surrender, of healing, health, and service.

We will go through some very dark and deep places; for we have not been buffered against pain, suffering, and the many tensions of the world.

But when God's will is done in our lives, we are provided with new and helpful resources with which to live sober and productive lives.

Furthermore, we are promised the presence of the Lord to be with us, and the will of God to be done in our lives.

But we must pray, "Not my will, but your will be done."

By so doing we prepare ourselves spiritually for God's grace to abound in our lives.

Am I praying for God's will to be done in my life? Am I turning my will and my life over to God's care and keeping?

God grant God's will to be done in and through me.

God's will for us is to grow.

WATCHING AND PRAYING

"Watch and pray so that you will not fall into temptation."—MATTHEW 26:41

Deep in our subconscious (and sometimes not so deep) is the memory of the "fix" and the desire to do it again.

Those who are aware of this reality tend to say, "I don't think about drinking, but I assume that my mind is thinking about it whether I am aware of it or not."

One of our brothers says, "All of a sudden there I was with a glass in hand, a glass of wine. And I asked myself, 'What are you doing?' And I said to myself . . . 'I'm drinking again.' "

The desire to use is always present in our conscious or subconscious minds.

Therefore it is prudent to "watch and pray so that you will not fall into temptation."

Am I being watchful over my sobriety? Am I being faithful to my prayer life?

God grant that I may be watchful and prayerful in all aspects of my life.

Two things we cannot overdo are watchfulness and prayer.

July 3

UNDERSTANDING AND ACCEPTING WEAKNESS

"The spirit is willing, but the body is weak."—MAT-
THEW 26:41

A host of body cells have been conditioned to
crave certain additives, whatever they may be; and
those cells are going to scream for gratification.

"I am thirsty! Give me a drink! I am hungry! Give
me some sugar! Give me my fix!"

As we progress in our sobriety, the cells learn that
something is changing, when finally they are put in
their place. And, when they are not listened to over
a period of time, they quiet down. But never do they
give up; not with the old ego still trying to direct the
traffic.

We must be aware of this reality: Our spirit is
willing to do what is best, but the old automatic
response mechanisms are still in place, waiting for
the first opportunity to get their own way.

Am I aware of my true condition? Do I understand
the depth and seriousness of my disease?

*God grant that the desires of my spirit may be
stronger than the desires of my body.*

Good intentions are good, but they don't always
work.

PUTTING ASIDE THE SWORDS

"Put your sword back in its place."—MATTHEW 26:52

Sometimes we approach life like a war. We gird up and get out the hardware for battle; gritting our teeth trying to be brave, trying to bluff our way into a lasting sobriety.

We may see our disease like an enemy that has to be struck down—as David mutilated Goliath, or as Peter tried to protect his Lord with a sword.

However, such tactics don't work for sobriety. In fact, such attempts lead to near-certain failure.

We are asked to accept our condition for what it is, and ourselves for the way we are.

We are asked to put up our swords.

We are neither to run away nor stay and fight. We simply are invited to give up, to accept our condition and surrender our lives into the care and keeping of God.

Because that is the way for a lasting sober life.

Am I laying aside my swords? Am I accepting my condition and surrendering myself to the will and power of God?

God grant that I may surrender to sobriety.

Fighting for sobriety may sound good, but it isn't. Surrendering to it is

July 5

TRYING A NEW WAY OF LIFE

> *"All who draw the sword will die by the sword."*
> —MATTHEW 25:52

In our recovery, we are looking for the development of new attitudes, new ways to approach old problems.

For instance, the old attitude of aggressiveness is replaced by acceptance and surrender.

No longer are we attempting to fight our way through. We are asking God to lead us.

Because when we remain aggressively defensive we place undue pressure on our sought-for sobriety.

Jesus told Peter to put up his sword because he knew the consequences of wielding the sword.

Jesus was teaching Peter a new way of life.

We also are learning a new way of life. Our old aggressive behavior no longer is destroying us.

Where once we were drawing our swords, trying to fight our way out of conflict, now we are dropping defensiveness and letting God show us the way.

Are my attitudes changing? Am I trying a new way of life?

God grant that my way of life may continue to change for the better.

Developing a new way of life is the primary project.

ACCEPTING POWER AND AUTHORITY

"All authority in heaven and on earth has been given to me."—MATTHEW 28:18

Christ is our power source.

From Christ, and through the Holy Spirit he sends to us, we gain authority over all that would destroy us.

And this is of great significance since we vividly remember our powerlessness; remember when we were trapped in our affliction, when we couldn't stop using.

The authority and power needed to help us in our recovery is a power greater than ourselves.

Paying close attention to our relationship with Christ—while doing all in our power to strengthen it—is the very best we can do for ourselves.

Am I accepting the power and authority of Christ into my life? Am I making use of that power and authority in my recovery?

God grant that I may accept the power and authority of Christ into my life.

True power and authority never arises from below. It comes down from above.

July 7

CARRYING THE MESSAGE

"Go and make disciples of all nations."—MATTHEW 28:19

Carrying the message isn't a matter of success or failure, because we are responsible for neither. It is simply a matter of doing what is very helpful to ourselves, and what we hope will be helpful to others: sharing our strength and hope.

"Discipleship" in the case of recovering Christians is allegiance and service to Christ.

Christ is the beginning and the end of our salvation, of our recovery.

Our first loyalty is to Christ. And true loyalty to Christ means offered service of ourselves to others.

Thus Christ becomes the real impetus for our carrying the message, as we practice the steps of recovery in all our affairs.

Making disciples of all nations means carrying the message of recovery—of faith, hope, and love.

Am I being a disciple of Christ? Am I carrying the good news of salvation to others?

God grant that I may carry the message of faith, hope, and love.

Carrying the message is the building of our sobriety.

BEING OBEDIENT TO LOVE

"Teaching them to obey everything I have commanded you."—MATTHEW 28:20

How do we teach love except that we first learn how to love?

And how do we learn to love except that we do the works of love, helping other people to live?

Obedience is doing what we are asked to do.

Yes, there are days when we don't feel like obeying the command to love one another. Yet it still is possible to do the works of love even when we don't want to, even when we are feeling sorry for ourselves, even when we are angry and upset.

We teach by example, by attraction rather than promotion.

And with true humility we allow ourselves to be enfolded by the love of Christ.

Am I obeying Christ's command to love and to serve? By my example am I teaching this commandment to others?

God grant that I may be obedient to love.

Being obedient to Christ is being obedient to love. Being obedient to love is being obedient to Christ.

July 9

BELIEVING THE PROMISE OF CHRIST

"And surely I will be with you always, to the very end of the age."—MATTHEW 28:20

We need the assurance of presence, because we cannot make it without support.

And if this is weakness, so be it.

The need remains a life-or-death matter.

We know about isolation and loneliness—about emptiness.

We sought our support the best way we knew how or were able. We could hear the bottle say, "I will be with you always," but we also knew this was a lie.

But we had to believe something, or die.

Far better is it for us that we have Christ's promise to be with us all the way. For this is the assurance that really lasts and grows, once we have accepted the promise and have come to believe it.

There is no end to the presence of Christ who is our power for new life, new hope, and new joy.

Am I believing the promise of Christ to be with me always? Am I carrying that promise with me?

God grant that I may believe the promises of Christ.

Believing and living the promises of Christ will lead us into a lasting and growing sobriety.

LOOKING FOR CHRIST

And when they found [Jesus], they exclaimed, "Everyone is looking for you!"—MARK 1:37

We sense that we are not complete, in and of ourselves—or even when we are with one another in the fellowship of recovering people.

St. Augustine said that our souls do not come to rest until they find their rest in God. And this is true.

It's good to know what we are looking for, to know about our essential loneliness, where it comes from and what it's about.

We are like travelers on an ancient and foreign planet, pilgrims and strangers longing to go home.

The closest we can approach satisfaction for this longing is through Christ.

Christ lifts us when we fall, and carries us when we are too weak to walk.

Christ is the one we have always been looking for.

Am I aware of Christ in my daily life and living? Am I allowing Christ to help me along the way?

God grant that I may always find the Christ for whom my heart longs.

Knowing what you are really looking for builds a good sobriety.

July 11

BEING READY AND WILLING

> *A man with leprosy came to him and begged him on his knees, "If you are willing, you can make me clean."*
> —MARK 1:40

Didn't we finally come to a place of confession, hope, and trust?

"If you are willing, Lord, you can make me clean."

Didn't we know that we had to get cleaned up, because the way we were going was deadly?

And while nothing about the deadly way has changed, we are, thank God, in the process of being changed.

The Lord is able to help us stay clean and sober today; as long as we, like the leper, are ready.

Being "ready"—ready and willing to be clean of all that would keep us in bondage—is the secret to sobriety.

Am I ready and willing to be clean? Am I asking the Lord for help day by day?

God grant that I may be ready and willing to stay clean and sober today.

Readiness and willingness unlock the doors to sobriety and keep them open.

STAYING CLEAN

Filled with compassion, Jesus reached out his hand and touched the man. "I am willing," he said. "Be clean!"—MARK 1:41

When we are ready and willing to stay clean, Christ is ready and willing to help us do just that.

However, in the course of our sobriety, of staying sober, there are times when we are less ready and less willing—as consciously or subconsciously the old tunes begin to play again—the old feelings of uneasiness, emptiness, fear, worry, trepidation, little resentments, anger, loneliness.

We now know that we must be entirely willing to stay clean and sober, that we cannot do this by the week, month, or year—only one day at a time.

The Lord is always willing to be with us when we are willing—willing to be touched and kept clean.

Am I reaching for the help I need, one day at a time? Am I willing to have Christ touch my life, day by day?

God grant that I may reach for help when I need it, day by day.

Every-day willingness is the secret to a good sobriety.

BEING CLEAN FOR TODAY

Immediately the leprosy left him and he was cured.
—MARK 1:42

One night, while drinking, he decided that he would have to commit his beloved wife to a mental institution the next day. This made him very sad indeed, because, in his own way, he loved her so much.

After a night of sweating and shaking and near panic due to alcohol burn-off, his mind cleared and he saw the situation for what it really was.

Without saying anything to anyone, that very morning he voluntarily committed himself to an alcohol treatment center, realizing that he was the "crazy one," not his wife.

Immediately he had become sober—by the grace of God. But, like the leper in our story, it had taken him a long time to get to his healer and healing.

Am I grateful for my healing? Am I putting my healing to work?

God grant that I may stay clean and sober today.

Being clean just for today is being clean for life.

GOING HOME

> *He said to the paralytic, "I tell you, get up, take your mat and go home."*—MARK 2:10–11

No doubt the healed paralytic was filled with joy about his healing, but he also probably bumped into the unanticipated.

No longer could there be the same old excuses for not getting work done. After he was healed he had to carry his share of the duty.

So it is with us when we become sober. We have to face the need to change because that's what recovery is about. Change.

And change has to start with us.

We must concentrate on our own changing, not on change as we would like to see it in others.

And this new attitude makes "going home" quite a challenge, one we have to deal with each and every day: with God's help.

Am I accepting responsibility for my life? Are my attitudes and reactions changing little by little, day by day?

God grant that I may accept responsibility for my sobriety and life.

Getting sober is only the beginning of staying sober.

July 15

BEING WHAT WE ARE

> *"It is not the healthy who need a doctor, but the sick. I have not come to call the righteous, but sinners."*
> —MARK 2:17

We know what illusion, delusion, and false pride already have done to us, when we tried to go it alone; when we refused to admit that we needed help and healing.

Those who feel no such need have no need for the doctor.

But we feel the need, knowing full well that we need the doctor.

Christ is our soul's doctor.

Christ does for us what we cannot do for ourselves.

Christ sets us free from our obsessiveness, our compulsiveness; from the rulership of our addictions.

Denial of our disease and denial of our need for the doctor is a pitiful way to abstain.

Am I satisfied that each day I need help? Am I turning to Christ to receive the help I need to stay sober, one day at a time?

God grant that I may see my true condition and affirm it.

To be stubborn and proud is to be miserable and lost.

SUPPORTING UNITY

"If a kingdom is divided against itself, that kingdom cannot stand."—MARK 3:24

Unity, in our fellowships of recovering people, is the key to healthy and long-lasting sobriety.

Of course, there are going to be abrasive times within the fellowship, particularly when we revert to alcoholic thinking and acting.

But we have discovered that our fellowship is much stronger than anyone could have anticipated.

Governed only by the group conscience and prayer for God's will to be done in all our affairs, we are able to put aside our differences and work together for the common good.

We are aware of the fact that a kingdom divided against itself cannot stand, and that all kingdoms are fragile. That is why we pay such close attention to unity, letting nothing divide us into sectarian factions.

Am I supporting unity of the fellowship? Am I helping to build the fellowship of recovering persons?

God grant that I may support the unity of our fellowship.

United we stand. Divided we fall.

DOING THE WILL OF GOD

> *"Whoever does God's will is my brother and sister and mother."*—MARK 3:35

"The will of God" is helping one another to live sober lives through recovery, unity, and service.

Christ assures that we are his brothers and sisters as we do the will of God.

It is not always convenient to do the will of God. Sometimes it can be very demanding on our time, energy, and resources.

The phone may ring while we are eating or sleeping or visiting with friends, and we don't feel like responding. But respond we do, because we are being called to help someone in need.

Those of us who have made such calls for help know what it is to be served by a brother or sister in the fellowship.

Kinship with Christ is realized and developed as we help one another along the path of recovery, unity, and service.

Am I doing the will of God? Am I helping other people to live?

God grant that I may help other people to live.

Doing the will of God is helping one another to live.

LETTING YOUR LIGHT SHINE

"Do you bring in a lamp to put it under a bowl or a bed? Instead, don't you put it on its stand?"—MARK 4:21

We have a tradition known as anonymity—being quiet—not drawing needless attention to ourselves as recovering people.

Originally this tradition was established when alcoholics were looked on as weaklings and hopeless.

But today the climate is changing. Famous people regularly are becoming part of our recovering fellowship—speaking openly about their disease, about their recovery and the value of our fellowship.

Nevertheless anonymity is vital to sobriety because proudly broadcasting our new life can resurrect latent grandiosity and blow our recovery.

Yet we do not want to hide our gratitude. Always we should remember: "Attraction rather than promotion."

Am I hiding any of the gifts of sobriety—new faith, hope, love, joy, serenity?

God grant that I may let my sobriety shine.

Let it shine—let it shine—all the time.

CELEBRATING THE MYSTERIES OF GOD

> *"Whatever is hidden is meant to be disclosed, and whatever is concealed is meant to brought out into the open."*—MARK 4:22

People are becoming more and more aware of the miracles of recovery that happen each and every day.

No longer are the miracles of God in the fellowship a secret.

No longer can it be denied that, by the grace of God and the fellowship of recovering people, miracles continue to happen on a daily basis.

People who were lost are found, people who were down are up, people who were dead are alive.

As has been said so many times, "The secret is out!"

Our faith in God is not being hidden.

Am I grateful for the mercies of God? Am I celebrating the mysteries and miracles of God with thanksgiving?

God grant that the good news of recovery is spread abroad.

Celebrating the mysteries and miracles of God is the adrenaline of recovery.

GIVING AND GETTING

> *"With the measure you use, it will be measured to you."*—MARK 4:24

This is no secret: We get as much out of our recovery as we put into it.

There is no other way to make progress in the program except by entering it fully, holding nothing back.

This means, among other things, that we go to meetings, read our books, pray, meditate, and offer ourselves in service to others.

In one sense, ours is a selfish program: We have to take care of our own sobriety first, before we think about trying to help others who suffer.

By paying attention to ourselves first, we are positioned to help others.

Am I giving myself to Christ? Am I giving of myself to others?

God grant that I may be a giving person.

Happiness is giving. Giving is joy.

July 21

GIVING THANKS FOR THE MIRACLES OF GROWTH

"This is what the kingdom of God is like. A man scatters seed on the ground. Night and day, whether he sleeps or gets up, the seed sprouts and grows, though he does not know how."—MARK 4:26–27

The miracles and mysteries of God abound every day as we watch ourselves and others grow in sobriety.

While it is clear that we must stay active in our recovery—working the program—it also is true that we are growing spiritually in a quiet way, being fed abundantly by God's gifts of grace.

God's grace is like seed spread on the ground, working in our hearts, setting down roots and growing, even while we are resting.

This is the mystery of growth and development that keeps us in awe and wonder.

Little by little the sprouts of new growth begin to surface, piercing our defense systems, like plants breaking through concrete.

Am I seeing the miracles of growth in my life? Am I giving thanks for the miracles of growth?

God grant that I may see the miracle of growth in my life.

Growth and development are miracles of God.

LIVING THE DESIGN

> *"All by itself the soil produces grain—first the stalk, then the head, then the full kernel in the head."*
> —MARK 4:28

Soil is the conduit for life energy and growth. But in order to energize life, soil must have nutrients on which the seeds can feed—first the stalk, then the head, and then the full kernel in the head. That's the design, and it cannot be changed.

So also is it with the recovery process. First the stalk: the desire to stop using.

The design for recovery is one step at a time.

When the steps are done progressively, honestly, and without modification, recovery is the result. A full kernel.

Sobriety is like a plant in need of nutrients.

The soil is God's Holy Spirit from whom we gain all the needed nutrients to produce the full kernels of sobriety—faith, hope, and love.

Am I accepting the design for recovery? Am I allowing myself to grow?

God grant that I may grow into a strong and lasting sobriety.

Understanding the design for recovery and following it is the secret to a long, lasting, and joyful sobriety.

July 23

STILLING THE TEMPESTS

He got up, rebuked the wind and said to the waves, "Quiet! Be still!" Then the wind died down and it was completely calm.—MARK 4:39

With his disciples Jesus embarks and quickly falls asleep, while his friends man the boat. A vicious and frightening storm arises, causing the disciples to cry out for Jesus to save them. "Don't you care if we drown?" they shout at Jesus, shaking him awake. Isn't that the way it seems to us in the midst of our storms, when the pressures are so intense? Does anyone care?

Remember the feelings of isolation and fear?

Remember: "We admitted we were powerless, that our lives had become unmanageable!"

Remember: "We made a decision to turn our wills and our lives over to the care and keeping of God!" And the Lord said to the storms, "Quiet! Be still!"

Remember: We began to work our program for recovery, and a new stillness entered our lives.

Do I hear Him saying, "Quiet! Be still!"? Are the storms within me subsiding?

God grant that my inner storms may be quieted.

God does for us what no other power can do.

COMING TO BELIEVE

He said to his disciples, "Why are you so afraid? Do you still have no faith?"—MARK 4:40

Do we have no faith? Sometimes.

Do we have very little faith? Often.

Do we forget what God has done in the past to save us? We do.

Do we want to believe God and be strong in our faith? Of course.

We are not perfect. Far from it.

But we are making progress. Trust is building. Hope is dawning. Love is growing.

Sometimes we even jump in all the way, believing God without reservation—committing ourselves totally to God's care and keeping.

Those are beautiful times, when the storms are stilled and we are set free from fear.

Amazing grace! We are coming to believe God.

Is my faith in God growing? Am I coming to believe God a little more, day by day?

God grant that I may come to believe Christ completely.

Believing Christ is like muscle building. It has to be practiced day by day.

July 25

BEING SET FREE

"Come out of this man, you evil spirit!"—MARK 5:8

Remember what it was like during those nightmarish times when it seemed as though we were possessed by demons? And perhaps we were.

We did things beyond comprehension, things we never would consider doing when sober.

We were beside ourselves.

Then something miraculous happened. We became sober.

This was the miracle that started a chain of miracles yet to come, one of which is like an exorcism. "Evil spirits" are addressed and dealt with, one at a time: the evil spirits of resentment, envy, sloth, impatience, and a myriad of others, each addressed by a power greater than ourselves, restoring us to sanity.

We become enabled to say, "Come out!" And by God's grace each character defect or evil spirit begins to loosen its grip on our lives.

Are my character defects being dealt with?

God grant that I may be set free from bondage to self.

Freedom from bondage to self is freedom to live abundantly.

GIVING GLORY TO GOD

> *"Go home to your family and tell them how much the*
> *Lord has done for you, and how he has had mercy on*
> *you."*—MARK 5:19

It's OK to be proud of ourselves and our achieve-
ments in gaining and sustaining our sobriety—as
long as we give God the glory for having empowered
us.

If we are confused about this and are boastful of
"our" accomplishments, we endanger the quality of
our sobriety, if not sobriety itself.

Real honest-to-goodness pride is self-affirmation,
where once there was self-defamation.

We don't need any more self-defamation. We do
need a lot of affirmation.

Giving glory to God is essential, letting other people know where our power is coming from.

God is our healer.

Let us give glory to God.

Am I humbly grateful for all blessings received? Am
I giving glory to God?

God grant that I may be humbly grateful.

Pride really does come before the fall.

July 27

BEING TOTALLY ACCEPTED

> He said to her, "Daughter, your faith has healed you.
> Go in peace and be freed from your suffering."—MARK
> 5:34

Sometimes it takes years before sobriety finally materializes. Why this is we don't really know, except to say that we were not ready.

When we are ready to change and be changed, positive things begin to happen.

When we finally humble ourselves before the Lord, praying only for God's will to be done and the power to carry it out, positive things begin to happen. This was the case of the woman in our story.

She fell at Jesus' feet, trembling with fear.

Would he, like others, turn away with anger and disgust? She didn't know for sure.

But Christ accepted her in her condition, without qualification. And so it is with us.

Because we belong to him.

Am I accepting myself as Christ accepts me? Am I allowing Christ to make me whole?

God grant that I may be clean and sober, whole and healthy.

Being cleansed is being clean, is being sober, is being alive and well.

BELIEVING—NOT FEARING

"Don't be afraid: just believe."—MARK 5:36

Because of pervasive fear we often are unable to take risks that hold promise for new life, new hope, and new joy.

Our Lord asks, invites, urges us to believe him, to live the life he has set before us by his own example, a life of giving love, sacrifice, and service.

Our Lord tells us not to be afraid, to trust God completely; believing that the will of God always is in our favor.

But we hesitate. We think it over and doubt, because we are afraid of the cost. We retreat, or hold tightly to what we have and think is ours, because we are afraid that we will lose more than we may gain. We try to play it safe, but by so doing we are the losers.

To all of this our Lord says, "Don't be afraid, just believe." Simplistic as that sounds, it works—when we are ready.

Am I believing God? Is my fear lessening?

God grant that I may believe and not be afraid.

Fear rejects faith just as faith dispels fear.

GETTING UP AND GETTING GOING

"I say to you, get up!"—MARK 5:41

The little girl was assumed dead, and people were wailing. But Jesus asked, "Why all this commotion and wailing? The child is not dead but asleep." This describes our spiritual condition while we are using: "not dead but asleep".

Then comes the command, "Get up!" And God be praised, we miraculously arise.

How did we manage to get up, to arise?

Did we do it on our own power with the strength of our own will? Is that how we got sober?

Or was it something else: a power greater than ourselves that lifted us up from our death beds and gave us new life?

Of course, we know the answer to such questions: "Not by my own reason or strength" but by the power of God!

Am I getting up and getting going? Am I taking one step at a time?

God grant that I may get up and get going, one step at a time.

When you get up and get going, you have a very good chance of getting there.

BEING ASTONISHED

> *Immediately the girl stood up and walked around
> . . . At this they were completely astonished.*—MARK
> 5:42

In our using days we were unconscious, spiritually
and emotionally and, sometimes, physically.

When we honestly recall our past and compare it
with the present, we are astonished.

This astonishment grows as we become more conscious of how it was, what happened to us, and how
it is now.

Thanks to the grace of God, we now are on our
feet.

Each day, as we reflect on the progress experienced in our program for recovery, we become ever
more astonished. And others are also astonished,
amazed how this change, this new birth, came about.

Am I astonished by what God is doing in and
through me? Am I grateful for the new life that is
mine to have?

*God grant that I may be astonished, thrilled, and
filled with gratitude for my salvation.*

Being surprised and astonished by God's grace is the
energy of a good recovery.

July 31

ANSWERING A CALL

> *Calling the Twelve to him [Jesus] sent them out two by two and gave them authority over evil spirits.*
> —MARK 6:7

Today let us briefly think about making a twelfth-Step call, carrying the message to someone who is suffering, answering a call for help.

The question is not whether we are going to be able to do anything to turn the course of events for the person involved—in and of ourselves we cannot change people.

However, when we believe that we are being called and sent, we fare much better. We are much more relaxed and helpful.

When we answer a call and are being sent to help, let us remember that we are not the ones who are doing the work.

Rather, God is working in and through us.

So we take no credit for success or seeming failure.

Am I answering the call to service? Am I going where God wants to send me?

God grant that I may accept every mission to which I am called and sent.

Answering a call to serve is the best answer there is.

BEING STRAIGHT AND CLEAN

> *And he promised her with an oath, "Whatever you ask I will give you, up to half of my kingdom."*—MARK 6:23

King Herod promises his wife's daughter her heart's desire if she would dance for him and his friends.

Obviously, Herod was drunk with wine, even promising "up to half of my kingdom," which is a lot for some belly dancing and, no doubt, a few extra favors.

For some of us these sorts of promises may sound familiar.

We may remember—or choose to forget—what it was like when we did virtually anything to satisfy our appetites of spiritual, emotional, and physical depravity.

But now that is over and done with.

Am I being true to my higher self? Am I being straight and clean with myself and others?

God grant that I may be straight and clean in all that I do.

Being straight and clean is much easier than being otherwise.

August 2

HONORING GOD

> *"These people honor me with their lips, but their hearts are far from me."*—MARK 7:6

One thing is certain: A good sobriety cannot be developed and maintained by lip service to God or our program for recovery.

While this should be obvious to anyone involved in the program for recovery, it still eludes us.

Nothing is more destructive to our growth and sobriety than hypocrisy, the wearing of masks—particularly masks of false piety.

Masks keep us from being straight about who we are, prevent others from seeing us, set up barriers, and make true fellowship impossible.

In working our program we come to understand how necessary and vital it is for us to be absolutely honest with ourselves, with others, and with God if we are going to develop and maintain a healthy sobriety.

Am I accepting myself the way I am? Am I honoring God?

God grant that I may lay aside my masks and honor God.

Absolute honesty is the best way to be your own real self and to honor God.

BEING FREE AND ACCEPTING

> *"They worship me in vain; their teachings are but rules taught by men."*—MARK 7:7

We can go through the motions of recovery by playing with spirituality: repeating prayers without reflecting on them, talking about service work and not doing it, thinking that rules and regulations are the most important part of a good and decent recovery program.

We may be tempted to establish rules and regulations for membership in our fellowship—beyond the simple willingness to stop drinking.

However, experience has taught that recovery is something other than rules and regulations, or teachings "taught by men."

Recovery is physical, mental, and above all, spiritual.

And there can be no rule making about this.

Am I being free and accepting? Or am I trying to make rules and regulations for others to follow?

God grant that I may be free and accepting of myself and others—just as we are.

Rules and regulations do not constitute sobriety. Never have, never will.

August 4

SERVING THE COMMAND TO LOVE

> *"You have let go of the commands of God and are holding on to the traditions of men."*—MARK 7:8

We may be experts on the traditions of AA, experts on the Twelve Steps of the program.

We may think we know all the answers, and be missing a healthy sobriety.

We know that some of the simplest souls are growing in the program. But they come to the program, God be praised, with a humility that fills us with awe, wonder, and joy.

These "simple souls" have learned to love, and that's a mighty big difference. They only want to love and serve in return for their received gift of sobriety; living out an attitude of gratitude.

There is no way to replace such love; not with ideas, opinions, rules, regulations, or traditions. For love is the cornerstone of our sobriety: love of God, of self, of others.

Am I serving the command to love? Am I learning to give of myself to God and to others?

God grant that I may serve love.

Staying with God's command to love is staying sober.

Working from the Inside Out

> *"What comes out of a man is what makes him 'unclean.' For from within, out of men's hearts, come evil thoughts, sexual immorality, theft, murder, adultery, greed, malice, deceit, lewdness, envy, slander, arrogance and folly. All these evils come from inside and make a man 'unclean.' "*—MARK 7:20–23

We can change exterior situations somewhat. But nothing is really gained until our inner condition is changed: attitudes, dispositions, and desires.

Sobriety has to do with the inner condition, with the wishes of our heart and the true desire of our souls to be cleansed, relieved, and healed.

As our interior self and behavior change, those around us change their behavior toward us.

It is what comes out of us, from the inside, that makes a real and lasting difference for our recovery and newness of life.

Am I working on my recovery from the inside out? Am I doing something about my character defects?

God grant that I may work on myself from the inside out.

Sobriety, first of all, is a matter for the soul to take up and expedite.

August 6

BEING RESTORED

> *"I have compassion for these people . . . If I send them home hungry, they will collapse on the way, because some of them have come a long distance."*—MARK 8:2–3

Compassion is basic to our program—caring for one another, for others who suffer. For what Jesus says is true: "If I send them home hungry, they will collapse on the way, because some of them have come a long distance."

Many of us have come a long distance, through very rugged country. Also, many of us have been received with compassion, with love and care, by people who are committed to helping others heal—helping the dead to come back to life.

We remember how it was to be stranded, far away from home, with no one to help; until someone reached out and touched us, as we never before have been touched.

Am I being restored? Am I open to the feeding of the Lord?

God grant that I may be spiritually fed.

Being fed by the Lord is being given the bread of life that knows no end.

SHARING WHAT WE HAVE

> *"How many loaves do you have?"*—MARK 8:5

When Jesus fed the four and the five thousand, he started with existing resources: a few loaves of bread, a couple of fish.

He didn't say to his disciples, "Don't be silly. We must have more than that."

Rather, he blessed what he had to work with, and the feeding took place until everyone was fed to overflowing.

We don't know precisely what happened.

Perhaps the people began to share what they had hidden in their garments, where bread supplies were kept for long journeys, when they saw the willingness of a small boy to share all he had.

The real miracle for us is that of sharing, something many of us were very hesitant to do, even though we pretended otherwise.

Am I sharing what has been given to me as a gift? Am I holding anything back?

God grant that I may share all that has been given to me as a gift.

Sharing is not a sideline endeavor for anyone wanting to stay sober.

August 8

BEING SATISFIED

The people ate and were satisfied.—MARK 8:8

This is an interlude for us, a kind of doxology for the love and grace of God.

People eat and are satisfied. This is a good description of what happens to us when we are participants in the program for recovery and in fellowship with our Lord.

God provides the impetus, the energy, the food for our souls; and we experience satisfaction that comes in the form of serenity, peacefulness, calmness, tranquility. Something very new, especially for people like us.

The miracle is enlarged through sharing what we have with others, and their sharing with us, sharing our strength and hope.

We become satisfied as we participate in our recovery and the recovery of others, in fellowship.

Am I being satisfied? Am I receiving more satisfaction than I expected, from working my program and being sober?

God grant that I may be happy and content with my sobriety.

Being truly sober is being truly satisfied.

SEEING, HEARING, AND REMEMBERING

"Do you have eyes but fail to see, and ears but fail to hear? And don't you remember?"—MARK 8:18

Gaining lasting sobriety is based on remembrance of how it was, what it was like back then, and how it is to see the miracles of God at work in our lives today.

When we fail to see and hear what has happened—where we have been and what it was like—we also fail to see and hear the grace of God in our lives. This results in a lack of gratitude and joy.

Jesus had to ask his disciples if they remembered his feeding of the hungry. Their preoccupation with self got in the way.

In the program we continue to stress that we must not forget how it was with us.

Neither dare we forget how the grace of God lifted us out of the pits when we absolutely could not help ourselves.

Are my eyes open to God's love? Am I seeing and remembering the miracles of God in my life?

God grant that I may see, hear, and remember.

Seeing, hearing, and remembering the miracles of God is the three-fold secret of a lasting sobriety.

UNDERSTANDING

> *"Do you still not understand?"*—MARK 8:21

It has been said that we alcoholics and addicts are slow learners, and in some areas of our lives this is true. It's not that we are stupid. It's just that our minds are a bit bent out of shape, with the old stubbornness still at work.

Not unlike other people, perhaps.

But to stay sober we have to be more aware of ourselves than others.

In our recovery we have to go over the same territory many times. Over and over again, with the simplest things:

Like "easy does it" and "one day at a time."

Or this very simple truth: "If you don't drink, you won't get drunk."

Am I understanding how God's grace is working in my life? Am I putting the puzzles of my life and living together?

God grant that I may come to an ever deepening understanding of how I am put together and how sobriety works.

Understanding how sobriety works never comes easily, which is also why it's so exciting once it happens.

EXPERIENCING CHRIST

> *"Who do people say I am?"*—MARK 8:27

As Christians we have come to our own experience of Jesus. And, for each of us the experience of him is different.

We all have our own idea about him, who and what he is to us, even when we are using identical words to describe him, and his relationship to us.

The experience of Christ, knowing him as we alone know him, is unique to each of us.

And for some of us it has become abundantly clear that our program for recovery has evolved out of this person whom we know as Lord and Savior.

Who is Jesus?

Is he not the Generator and Sustainer of our sobriety?

Is he not the Generator of new life, new hope, and new joy?

Do I know Christ as my friend and savior? Am I staying close to him?

God grant that I may experience Christ as my Lord and savior.

Christ is the generating force of all creation and sobriety.

August 12

ANSWERING FOR OURSELVES

"Who do you say I am?"—MARK 8:29

We have to speak our own minds and hearts and convictions.

When we come to the person of the Christ, it is for each of us to decide, in our own way and time, who this person is.

When we answer this question, "Who do you say I am?" our lives can take on a more specific focus.

It is not for us to judge others as being wrong and ourselves as being right. It is for us to be certain about ourselves and our relationship to the Christ, whatever that relationship may be.

It's not a question of what others think or say, but what we think and say for ourselves.

Others cannot do for us what we must do for ourselves, cannot answer the questions of the heart for us.

"Who do you say I am?"

The answer belongs to each of us.

Am I stating my position clearly? Am I answering important questions for myself?

God grant that I may answer for myself.

Answering for ourselves is the only answer.

FOLLOWING THE CHRIST

> *"If anyone would come after me, he must deny himself and take up his cross and follow me."*—MARK 8:34

Then, one day, the time came to decide whether we were going to deny ourselves our pacifiers and take hold of life in another way.

Putting aside the bottle or the drugs was not enough in and of itself. Something new had to be added, something more than physical abstinence: a new life of faith, hope, and love, a new willingness to deny ourselves pacifiers.

Christ offers us the new way of life that satisfies, that provides an eternal sobriety of heart, mind, and spirit.

But, to have that way of life, we must consciously deny ourselves self-destructive behavior, lay aside negative attitudes.

This means that we are ready to bear whatever is required to keep us honest, upright, and committed to a new way of life.

Am I putting aside my pacifiers? Am I following Christ?

God grant that I may earnestly follow Christ.

Following Christ isn't painless, nor is it ever futile.

August 14

SEEING SUDDENLY

> *Suddenly, when they looked around, they no longer saw anyone with them except Jesus.*—MARK 9:8

Suddenly we looked around and nobody was there, not even ourselves.

Dreaded loneliness engulfed us: a sense of having been abandoned by God and our fellows.

Then one day, miraculously and *suddenly* we put aside our substances, the magic potions that were meant to help us know and do all that is right and good; potions which actually cluttered, confused, and destroyed.

Suddenly we began to see what had been hidden, and Christ began coming into focus.

Suddenly we began to grow in our sobriety, into peace, serenity, and joy.

Suddenly we become involved with miracles that haven't stopped happening to us, to this very day.

Am I seeing Christ as the miracle of my life? Am I growing in Christ, day by day?

God grant that I may see Christ in all of my life and living.

Suddenly we are involved with a growth process that knows no end.

BELIEVING

> *"Everything is possible for him who believes."*—MARK 9:23

Believing that everything is possible is not new for us. We did it all the time.

We believed that if we drank more we would feel better.

Our rotten self-image, even hatred of self, kept us locked in a no-win situation.

Now, however, we are better able to believe something new.

For instance, our coming to believe that we truly are children of God lifts us out of our unhappy feelings about ourselves, about others, and about God. Coming to believe that we are worth something, not as superstars, but simply as humble servants, makes living exciting.

Am I believing that all things are possible for me? Am I being positive about my life now and my life to come?

God grant that I may believe that all things are possible for me.

What is possible is the impossible.

August 16

BEING LAST AND BEING FIRST

> *"If anyone wants to be first, he must be the very last, and the servant of all."*—MARK 9:35

No longer are we striving to be more or less than we are.

No longer are we trying to push ourselves to the head of the line at the expense of someone else.

But neither are we invalidating ourselves, paying no attention to our own needs.

We begin to discover the vitality and importance of serving the greater good, rather than self serving.

We begin to see what it means to be a free human being, a soul released from the paralysis of self-centeredness.

Becoming the servant, we discover what it really is to be first.

Helping others to live, we find new life, hope, and joy.

This is most certainly true.

Am I a servant? Am I extending myself in behalf of others?

God grant that I may be the servant.

The true treasures of life are found where least expected.

BEING AT PEACE

"Be at peace with each other."—MARK 9:50

The life of an addict is an insane struggle of needless tension, strife, and war, with all serious attention fixed on self-gratification.

When Jesus asks us to be at peace with one another, he is asking us, first of all, to be at peace with ourselves.

For we will never be at peace with others unless we are first at peace with ourselves.

However, we do not suddenly and everlastingly fall into a state of peacefulness with ourselves, with others, and with God.

There are things we must do to experience peace: accept our condition, surrender our egos, turn our will and our lives over to God, and work our program in its totality.

"Half-measures availed us nothing," as the Big Book says.

Am I becoming peaceful? Am I learning to be at peace with myself, with others, and with God?

God grant me the gift of peace.

Being at peace is the ultimate gift of sobriety—the gift of God.

BEING UNITED

"And the two will become one flesh."—MARK 10:8

Unity is the fundamental design of creation, and of our recovery.

God has not designed the creation to be separated any more than a wife and husband are meant to be separated; or one human being from the entire family of God.

And this also is meant for the church.

"One holy and apostolic church"—the communion of saints.

Unity.

Oneness.

Synergism.

This is the way we are healed in the body of Christ and the fellowship of recovering persons.

True unity is the spiritual unity we find in our common purpose to stay sober and serve.

Am I united with myself, with others, with God? Am I serving the unity of spirit?

God grant that I may be in unity with myself, with others, with God.

Being together is better than being apart, because being apart is being nowhere.

STAYING CLOSE

> *"What God has joined together, let man not separate."*—MARK 10:9

Jesus is speaking about marriage, about being true to ourselves and true to others.

This also can apply to anything God has brought together, binding it in love—such as ourselves and our sobriety.

We have been joined into the life of sobriety, with all of its responsibilities and privileges:

Responsibilities to nurture the gifts offered and received.

Privileges of new relationships that come through our being sober, and leading sober lives.

We have been *brought* into a deeper closeness with ourselves, with others, and with God.

Christ's desire for us is that we never again become separated human beings, separated from ourselves, from others, from God.

Am I staying close to Christ? Am I staying close to others?

God grant that I may not be separated from myself, from others, from God.

Being separated is being alone, is being miserable.

RECEIVING AND ENTERING

> *"I tell you the truth, anyone who will not receive the kingdom of God like a little child will never enter it."*
> —MARK 10:15

This is absolutely true: Without the gift of true humility and the wonderment of a child, a mature and lasting sobriety is difficult, if not impossible.

To enter the kingdom of God we must be receptive to the gifts of God: the gifts of expectation, anticipation, trust, hope, and joy.

To enter the kingdom we must lay aside all resistance of mind, body, and spirit.

To enter the kingdom we must be ready and willing to go through every door God opens for us.

Receiving and entering God's kingdom is our new opportunity each day. One day at a time.

Am I laying aside my resistance? Am I receiving and entering God's kingdom of new life, new hope, new joy?

God grant that I may be as a little child, to receive and enter the kingdom of new life, new hope, and new joy.

Being God's little child is being alive and well.

BEING TRULY BLESSED

And he took the children in his arms, put his hands on them and blessed them. —MARK 10:16

When we enter the program for recovery, we must become as little children who don't know their way:

As little children who have to be held, now and then;

As little children who need to be blessed by affirmation;

As little children who need encouragement.

In recovery we begin to see ourselves as children, but not as childish. We affirm our need to be held once in a while and blessed—accepted and forgiven.

We begin to see that to be truly blessed is to be in a childlike attitude, open and receptive.

When the once-hard spirit softens, guilt and shame begin to crumble, to melt away.

We begin to feel secure in the care and keeping of our Lord.

Am I allowing myself to be truly blessed? Am I releasing myself into the care and keeping of Christ.

God grant that I allow myself to be truly blessed.

Being held and blessed is to be released and renewed.

Disbanding "Good" and "Bad"

> *"Why do you call me good? No one is good—except God alone."*—MARK 10:18

We remember, from childhood, words like "good" and "bad". And we bring these words with us into adulthood.

Many of us never really made the grade of being good.

So some of us specialized in being "bad."

Our Lord, however, never allowed himself to get pulled into this contest.

When someone said to him, "Good teacher," he rejected the label. That same person might also have said, "Bad teacher."

Jesus left the word "good" to apply to God alone.

Perhaps this means that we can also disregard the words "good" and "bad" when referring to ourselves or others.

Am I accepting myself the way I am? Am I accepting others the way they are?

God grant that I may love and accept myself the way I am.

Trying always to be "good" causes a pain that doesn't go away by itself.

ABIDING THE COMMANDMENTS

"You know the commandments."—MARK 10:19

The truth is that we really do know the difference between doing what is right and wrong for ourselves.

We know it intuitively.

What is outlined in the commandments, as a way of life, is the knowing and doing of God's will:

Have no other gods before God. (First things first)

Do not take the name of the Lord God in vain. (Watch your tongue)

Remember the Sabbath day to keep it holy. (Get some rest and pray)

Honor your father and mother. (Love, forgive, and bless)

Don't kill. (Bless rather than curse)

Don't commit adultery. (Be true to yourself)

Don't steal. (Honor your integrity)

Don't lie. (Build trust)

Don't covet. (Be content with what God has given)

Am I being honest with myself and others? Am I living the commandments of God?

God grant that I may live the commandments, with love.

The greatest commandment is love.

GOING THE WHOLE WAY

"One thing you lack. Go, sell everything you have and give to the poor, and you will have treasure in heaven. Then come, follow me."—MARK 10:21

Sobriety into a lasting and fruitful recovery is an all-or-nothing proposition; just as Jesus asked for an all-or-nothing commitment from those who chose to follow him.

Whatever stands in the way of our sobriety must be appropriately dispensed with.

Completely.

Utterly.

With no tentativeness.

With no holding back.

Following Jesus.

Doing whatever he wants us to do, in obedience to our Lord's commands.

Leaving behind all that is harmful to us.

Am I taking Jesus seriously? Am I ready to separate from everything that stands in the way of my recovery?

God grant that I may separate myself from all that threatens my sobriety.

Only when we divest ourselves of fearful egoistic attachments and crippling addictions do we begin to find new life, new hope, and new joy.

BEING SAD

He went away sad, because he had great wealth.
—MARK 10:22

The rich young man wanted to have his cake and eat it too—wanted to be affirmed as being perfect in his love of God.

But Jesus said he had to divest, which left the young man saddened.

To stay on the pathway of recovery, and not be left saddened, we give up, once and for all the illusion that we are in control, that we can ever use again.

We surrender ourselves into God's care and keeping without resentment, regret, discontent, or sadness.

We know that we are where we belong, doing that which is life-giving and best for us.

We know and believe that we are where God our Lord wants us to be.

Am I surrendered to God in Christ? Am I satisfied with spiritual progress rather than perfection?

God grant me the gift of surrender.

Sadness leaves when surrender begins.

August 26

MAKING THE IMPOSSIBLE POSSIBLE

"All things are possible with God."—MARK 10:27

Was it not hopeless as far as we and others were concerned?

And didn't hopelessness require even more sedation?

And, with sedation, more isolation?

Then, one day, as we so often must remind ourselves, a light went on.

Not a huge bright light, but a little flicker we had not previously seen, and we were drawn to it.

So we quit playing God. Almost.

We let God be God. Almost.

We became more conscious of God working in our lives as more of the impossible became possible.

Am I conscious of the presence of God in my life? Do I believe that God is able to make all things possible for me?

God grant that I may see the impossible becoming possible every day of my life.

Letting God be God is not the impossible task. Trying to be God is the impossible task.

LEAVING BEHIND

> *"We have left everything to follow you!"*—MARK 10:28

Self-pity arrives early in our sobriety. And it can hang on for longer than we care to admit: "Just think of all that I have had to give up!"

Then it's time to feel sorry for ourselves.

And resentful of people who didn't *have to* give up what we *have had to* sacrifice.

"We have left everything!"

We want others to recognize what we have done, especially those close to us: wives, husbands, children, fathers, mothers, coworkers—and especially God!

The truth is that all we have left behind is confusion, anger, fear, and dread.

We haven't left one thing that was doing us any good.

Am I resentful about where I am today? Am I looking back with regrets about what I have "given up" to get here?

God grant that I may be joyously satisfied with my sobriety.

Regrets leave us nowhere except left behind.

August 28

LIVING BETTER

> *"I tell you the truth, no one who has left home or brothers or sisters or mother or father or children or fields for me and the gospel will fail to receive a hundred times as much in this present age . . . and in the age to come, eternal life."*—MARK 10:30

What are we getting out of the program, when we are working it? Much more than ever could have expected or hoped for?

The rewards are new life, new hope, and new joy as we let go and let God: more confidence and contentment in the midst of turmoil.

What we are doing now—today—has much to do with what is to come, which makes this day, and the way we live it, extremely important.

With each day, and a life well lived, we experience more and more of the goodness and mercy of God.

Am I doing all I can today, to make this life better for myself and others? Am I leaving behind what is of no value to my spiritual growth and development?

God grant that I carry no excess baggage.

What is left behind stays behind.

Seeking What Is Best for Ourselves

"You don't know what you are asking."—MARK 10:38

At least two of Jesus' disciples didn't know what was best for them. They wanted more than they had: more power, more authority over others, more recognition, honor, and praise.

Sound familiar?

They wanted special attention from the Lord, special places in the kingdom of God, above the common folk.

Better for us to stay quietly in the shadows, removed from egoistic struggles in which the contests never cease.

Better still to devote our foremost attention to remaining sober, staying straight, and keeping clean.

Better for us to live in simple trust—resting ourselves in the care and keeping of our Lord.

Am I seeking what is best for me? Am I content with being quietly sober?

God grant that I may be quietly sober and content with myself.

Sometimes we want things that are not good for us, in spite of our best intentions to the contrary.

EXTENDING BEYOND OURSELVES

> *"For even the Son of Man did not come to be served,*
> *but to serve, and to give his life as a ransom for many."*
> —MARK 10:45

We are taught by our culture that we have something coming because of our "rights."

For instance, we may have the imagined "right" to expect someone to serve us, because of something special we have done, like getting sober.

Our program teaches, however, that we get sober for ourselves, not for anyone else.

So we don't expect to be served.

Rather, we respond to opportunities to extend beyond ourselves, to serve others.

By so doing we keep our sobriety, and strengthen it; which is in keeping with our Lord, who serves without hesitation, with no holding back.

Am I reaching beyond myself? Am I offering myself in service?

God grant that I may reach beyond myself in service.

Extending beyond ourselves is reaching for health and healing.

HEARING THE QUESTION

"What do you want me to do for you?"—MARK 10:51

The blind man knows he wants to see, but Jesus still asks, "What do you want me to do for you?"

And this is like it is for us.

Until we decide what it is we want for ourselves, nothing can be done about freeing us from fear, anger, resentment, and grief.

We don't stay sober until we ask for true sobriety—not with compliance, but in surrender.

A growing and lasting sobriety can't be forced on anyone.

Each day we should spell out what we want for ourselves, asking for health of spirit and healing.

"What do you want me to do for you?"

"Lord I want you to give me the gift of a sober life."

When we are specific about this, our sobriety is assured.

Am I asking God for a continuing sobriety? Am I trusting God to provide what I need to stay sober?

God grant that I may stay clean and sober today.

Being specific about wanting sobriety is being sober.

September 1

HAVING FAITH IN GOD

> *"Have faith in God."*—MARK 11:22

At our very best we are imperfect, bound to make mistakes.

Coming to accept our imperfections is a basic part of a good recovery.

One day we came to believe that a power greater than ourselves could restore us to sanity.

One day we came to believe that God in Christ is able to do for us what we cannot do for ourselves.

Now we know that faith in God is the answer to turmoil and confusion.

Nevertheless, we still seem to have to be reminded: *"Have faith in God."*

We have to be admonished, because we aren't perfect and because we forget.

Today, however, we are making progress in the matters of faith and life.

And this, by the power of God.

Do I have faith in God? Am I putting my faith to work one day at a time?

God grant me the gift of faith, one day at a time.

Having faith in God is doing the very best we can for our own benefit.

PRAYING AND ASKING

> *"Therefore I tell you, whatever you ask for in prayer, believe that you have received it, and it will be yours."*
> —MARK 11:24

True prayer is the expressed desire to be in concord with the will of God.

Praying and asking, coupled with the giving of thanks, is important for our sobriety.

We ask only for God's will to be done, and power to carry it out: "Not my will, but thy will be done."

More and more, as we pray for God's will to be done, we become interested in seeing what we can contribute to life.

More and more, God leads us into positions and places where such contributions materialize, where we can be of service to others.

When we pray for God's will to be done, we pray for the very best that ever can be granted.

Am I praying? Am I asking for God's will to be done in my life and the life of the world?

God grant: "Thy will be done in me."

Prayer is the door-opener to the Eternal.

September 3

LETTING GO OF RESENTMENT

> *"And when you stand praying, if you hold anything against anyone, forgive him, so that your Father in heaven may forgive you your sins."*—MARK 11:25

Resentment is a feeling of displeasure or indignation at something or someone because of real or imagined injury or insult.

Nothing is more destructive to our recovery.

Holding ill feelings binds us into negativity, preventing us from growing spiritually, hindering our recovery. Endangering our sobriety and lives.

Resentment eats at the body, mind, and spirit, giving rise to mental, physical, and spiritual disease. Resentment prevents us from dealing with ourselves and our own recovery.

If we are to experience a healthy sobriety we must thoroughly search out and confess all resentment, being willing to have God remove the ill feelings. Asking God to do so.

Am I holding any resentments? Am I willing to let go of them?

God grant that I may be free of resentment.

Letting go of resentment is letting go of self-will running riot.

AVOIDING ERROR

> *"Are you not in error because you do not know the Scriptures or the power of God?"*—MARK 12:24

We know something about the way things work in regards to recovery. In AA's Big Book there's an entire chapter entitled, "How It Works."

We also have the Bible, on which the Big Book is based.

The Bible is all about how it works—how salvation from fear, anger, and death materializes.

Not to know what is given us for our salvation is gross error.

The way to know the power of God is to tap into it, through the tools set before us: scripture and other related literature, prayer, meditation, meetings, and service.

Indeed, we do have access to the power of God.

Am I searching the scriptures? Am I staying close to Christ?

God grant that I may diligently search the scriptures, and find new life.

Daily reading of the scriptures, reflection, prayer, meditation, and service is the energy for a new way of life.

September 5

BEING ALERT

> *"Watch out that no one deceives you."*—MARK 13:5

Some have tried to prove that alcoholics can be taught to drink socially.

The truth is that we alcoholics never were social drinkers to begin with.

We drank for other reasons than "normal" people may drink.

We drank to escape, to get away from pain. And for a time it worked that way.

For us there is no such thing as one drink or social drinking.

We may be tempted by voices suggesting that we can be normal, "like other people"—drinking just for the fun of it, and not overdoing it.

But that is a lie.

Am I wishing that I could use again? Am I hearing voices saying that I can be moderate in these matters?

God grant that I may not deceive myself about myself.

Another drunk is only one drink away. So is the end of a life.

SEEING WHAT IS FALSE

"Many will come in my name, claiming, 'I am he,' and will deceive many."—MARK 13:6

Our "messiah/savior" wasn't even a person. It was a thing: a bottle, a prescription, a piece of cake, a snort of something.

The false prophet, we discovered, came from within, from our appetites: insatiable hungers for escape, comfort, illusion, serenity.

Our own false messiahs still beckon, still call, still point the way we wistfully want to go—into euphoria.

Then there are other false prophets who suggest that we can learn how to control our drinking if we do what they tell us, if we retrain ourselves.

Some of us would like to believe the voices; and some have tried the promise, only to discover what we already really know: It isn't true. It doesn't work.

Am I listening to the wrong voices? Am I wanting to believe what I already know to be false?

God grant that I may listen only to that which is true.

Truth endures and keeps us sober.

September 7

STANDING FIRM

> *"He who stands firm to the end will be saved."*—MARK 13:13

We can live the will of God.
We can believe God's promises.
We can be faithful in our discipleship.
Recovery, remember, is a day-by-day process.
Recovery is one day at a time, with no hesitation, no looking back, no regrets. And lots of gratitude.
Standing firm means the refusal of false voices and promises, listening to the still, small voice of God.
Standing firm means being united with others like ourselves, in a fellowship of strength and support.
Standing firm means keeping the faith, not in what we can do, but what God is able to do in and through us.
Standing firm is standing sober, soberly standing.
Standing firm is being grateful.

Am I standing firm? Am I grateful for my sobriety?

God grant that I may stand firm, with gratitude.

Standing firm is not standing rigid. Standing firm is standing free.

HOLDING ON TO THAT WHICH LASTS

> *"Heaven and earth will pass away, but my words will never pass away."*—MARK 13:31

We long for stability, something and someone on whom we can count.

Like anyone else we are aware of the transitoriness of life, how quickly it passes: Here today and gone tomorrow. It is natural and understandable then that we long for the eternal, that which lasts.

The life and teachings of our Lord grow in their validity more and more, day after day. The words of our Lord will never be outdated by time or circumstance.

We can trust them to be here forever.

Knowing this, we are able to take hold of that which lasts, take hold of that which strengthens our will and desire to be sober.

Stability rests in Christ Jesus our Lord, whose words never pass away; whose life and teachings keep us walking in the light.

Am I listening to the words of the Lord? Am I following his teachings?

God grant that I may listen and live the words of my Lord.

Listening, learning, and doing—the threefold way of sobriety.

September 9

BEING ON GUARD AND ALERT

"Be on guard! Be alert!"—MARK 13:33

Being alert to our condition, and the possibility of a slip, is essential. We are, seemingly by nature, susceptible to deception. For instance, the deceptive misbelief that a single drink cannot harm us.

There are false leaders who would have us believe that we can be reeducated as social drinkers. As a result, we may find ourselves becoming a bit careless about our sobriety, tinkering around with the idea that maybe we can get away with a drink now and then.

However, we have been warned that alcohol is cunning, baffling, and powerful, like any addictive substance. From personal experience we know this to be true, for we have fallen prey to its wizardry.

Sobriety calls for a sound defense against misleading illusions of infallibility—an alertness to all kinds of other evil that can hurt and destroy us.

Am I alert? Am I aware of the dangers that can befall me and my sobriety?

God grant that I may be aware of all dangers to my sobriety.

Not being on guard and alert is not being sober.

SHARING THE GIFTS OF CHRIST

"Take it; this is my body."—MARK 14:22

We are asked to participate in Christ's sacrifice—joining each with the other, and all of us with Christ.

Christ offers himself totally to us, so that through him we are enabled to let go of self-centeredness that has been destroying us.

United with Christ, we are empowered to live beyond ourselves, extended sacrificially in love and service to others—just as Christ is sacrificially extended toward us.

"Take and eat my body" means, "Take all of me. Utilize me. Devour me. Let me be in you. Let me serve you."

The gift of the Christ is like no other because it is total—with nothing held back. And the most exciting, wonderful part is that the offered gift is made to people such as ourselves.

Am I accepting the gifts of Christ day by day? Am I sharing the gifts with others?

God grant that I may accept and share Christ with others.

When we share Christ, we share life eternal.

September 11

CARRYING THE MESSAGE

> *"I must preach the good news of the kingdom of God to the other towns also, because that is why I was sent."*—LUKE 4:43

His disciples would have confined the ministry of Jesus to certain localities, and certain people.

But he knew that his good news needed to be carried to others, and so do we.

Going out to others with the good news of sanity in sobriety is an important part of our program.

We must not confine ourselves to our meeting rooms and "in" groups. We too are called and sent.

It was not by our own reason or strength that we came to believe or turn our wills and our lives over to the care of God.

By sharing the good news with others we keep our sobriety alive.

Am I carrying the message to others? Am I sharing what has been given to me?

God grant that I may carry the message of recovery to others.

Carrying the message to others is carrying it back to ourselves.

TRUSTING CHRIST TO HEAL

> *A man came along who was covered with leprosy.*
> *When he saw Jesus, he fell with his face to the ground*
> *and begged him, "Lord, if you are willing, you can*
> *make me clean."*—LUKE 5:12

Like the lepers and blind and crippled of old, we also are in line for rebirth into recovery. Day by day, one day at a time.

The leper had come to believe, and he had nothing to lose.

We too come to believe.

We too have nothing to lose.

We too have everything to gain: by turning to Christ and making ourselves available to him.

Christ doesn't ask us to beg, doesn't require that we fall down and worship him.

Christ asks only that we openly receive his love and offer it to others. For love, offered, is the master key to sobriety and to abundant life.

Am I trusting Christ's healing power? Am I permitting Christ to heal me?

God grant that I may keep myself open to the healing Christ.

Trusting Christ with our lives is staying sober.

September 13

AFFIRMING OUR FAITH

> *When Jesus saw their faith, he said, "Friend, your sins are forgiven."*—LUKE 5:20

We experience disability because of separation from God, which is sin.

Some of us are physically bent out of shape because of abusive behavior directed against our bodies; but our sins are forgiven.

Jesus saw the faith of people who brought a paralytic man to him for healing.

They came as a confessing community, placing their trust in the Lord.

So we also are brought, and bring others to Jesus, to our community of faith. We lay our burdens before the Lord, who tells us, "Your sins are forgiven."

And we experience forgiveness in the course of our recovery—more forgiveness than we ever could have hoped for or imagined possible.

Am I affirming my faith in Christ? Am I accepting the forgiveness of my sins?

God grant that I place my faith and trust in the forgiveness of sins, in life everlasting.

Forgiveness of sin is where true recovery begins.

BEING FILLED WITH AWE

They were filled with awe and said, "We have seen remarkable things today."—LUKE 5:26

The people saw what Jesus could do, and what he did—how he healed the hopeless, and gave new life to the dying.

And so do we.

These miracles of new life and hope are a regular, ongoing part of our fellowship.

We are in awe about what has happened to us: the impossible becoming possible, life rising up from death.

We are in awe about what is happening to others.

Like the people of old we can say, "We have seen remarkable things today."

We are filled with awe because of what God is doing in and through us.

Am I seeing the remarkable things God is doing? Am I giving thanks for the remarkable gifts of God given to me?

God grant that I may always be aware of remarkable things that come to pass in my life and the lives of others.

To be in awe and wonder is to be alive and well.

EXTENDING BEYOND OURSELVES

> *"If you love those who love you, what credit is that to you?"*—LUKE 6:32

Always there is the tendency to revert to tribalism, to serve those who serve us, love those who love us, who think and feel the way we do; vote as we do; have the same biases and prejudices.

However, in our program we meet many people who are hardly at all like we are. And some are obnoxious, perhaps like ourselves.

Nonetheless, we are called to love one another, in fellowship and outside the fellowship.

This is easier said than done.

Yet this is an essential part of our program:

Reaching out to all who suffer and loving the unlovable; loving those who are not able to return our love.

Loving as Christ loves us.

Am I extending beyond myself? Am I loving those who are unable to return my love?

God grant me the power to love the unlovable.

This business of loving is not as easy as we would like it to be.

Doing Good

> *"And if you do good to those who are good to you, what credit is that to you?"*—LUKE 6:33

It's easy to be good to those who are good to us, but what about doing good to a falling-down, obnoxious, foul-mouthed drunk?

That's another matter, and not too many of us are good at it.

An old saying says we should do at least one good turn a day for someone who doesn't know we are doing it. Anonymously.

Jesus prayed for those who mocked him at the cross: "Father forgive them."

Similarly, a time comes when we are called to return good for evil. This is not impossible, but it requires all the help we can get.

And our help comes from the Lord.

Am I being good to those who cannot be good to me? Am I doing good with no demands or qualifications?

God grant that I may do good without expecting a return.

God knows when we're doing good, and that is sufficient.

September 17

BEING MERCIFUL

"Be merciful."—LUKE 6:36

There is no end, no boundary, to the mercy of God.

While we were still sinners, Christ died for us.

Christ reached out, lifted us up, saved us from bondage and death. And that is the substance of mercy: someone doing something life-giving for us that we can't do for ourselves.

Now that we have been treated mercifully we are asked to be merciful to others.

This may mean something as simple as a smile, a handshake, a ride to a meeting, a telephone call, whatever; anything that welcomes suffering people into the fellowship and helps keep them there.

Mercy is the cup of cold water offered to the thirsty, and bread to the hungry.

Mercy is offering life to the dead.

Am I extending God's mercy to others? Am I offering what I am being given?

God grant that I may be merciful as mercy has been given me.

Mercy is the cornerstone of our recovery.

STAYING ON OUR OWN CASE

"Do not judge, and you will not be judged. Do not condemn, and you will not be condemned. Forgive, and you will be forgiven."—LUKE 6:37

Why do we have to be reminded of something so obvious—reminded over and over again?

One would think that we would know how things go: that if we judge others, we are going to be judged; that if we condemn others, we are condemning ourselves.

That to be forgiven we must forgive.

The essence of our program is to stay on our own case, and let others stay on theirs.

We mind our own store.

If and when we get on someone else with judgment or even condemnation, we are off our own case and in line for some painful repercussions.

Far better to concentrate on the positive, to live and let live.

Am I staying on my own program? Am I staying off the backs of others?

God grant that I may stay on my own case.

Judging and condemning others is judging and condemning ourselves.

Giving and Receiving

> *"Give, and it will be given to you. A good measure, pressed down, shaken together and running over, will be poured into your lap."*—LUKE 6:38

Everyone wants and needs a return on investment. Otherwise there would be no risk-taking.

So it is with abstinence, with our sobriety and progress in recovery.

The more we give, the more is given to us.

Not in wealth and material prosperity, as some would have us believe, but in spiritual growth and development—in sobriety, with new life, new hope, and new joy.

The longer we are in the program, and working it, the greater the blessings poured into our laps.

The more we give mercy, forgiveness, and love, the more we receive.

Another, and perhaps negative way of putting this: "What do you expect when you are not giving? A massive miracle that not even God can do? Getting blood out of a turnip?"

Am I giving? Am I receiving?

God grant that I may give and receive.

Giving builds the muscles of our sobriety.

BEING LED

> *"Can a blind man lead a blind man? Will they not both fall into a pit?"*—LUKE 6:39

That's how we were when we were still using—irrational and out of control.

We needed someone to lead us out of the darkness in which we had been far too long.

Because we were blind.

Because we couldn't read the road signs.

Because we had tried so long, so hard, and had failed to get sober.

But now we have someone to lead us, someone who is not blind, and someone who knows the way.

He says, "I am the way. I am the truth. I am the light you have been looking for."

We believe Christ.

We follow his leading.

We walk in his path.

And we don't fall into the pit.

Am I allowing myself to be led? Am I walking in the light?

God grant that I be led by Christ, into the light.

Christ knows the way, because Christ is the way.

September 21

BECOMING WHAT WE WANT TO BE

> *"No good tree bears bad fruit, nor does a bad tree bear good fruit."*—LUKE 6:43

There was something essentially out of kilter with us, and we couldn't on our own get straightened out.

We needed something more than better habits.

We needed to become new people.

We needed to be reborn, to become a good tree that could bear good fruit.

Then one day it was a new day for us. A new day of new beginnings.

Don't ask us how.

But suddenly we stepped over the line into a new place, into the gardens of God; where new life, new hope, and new joy were born anew in ourselves and others.

It was then that things began to change, because we were being cultivated and changed for the better.

Am I becoming what I want to be? Am I bearing good fruit?

God grant that I may be a good tree bearing good fruit.

Being a good tree is being in the right orchard, with the right gardener.

DOING WHAT WE SAY

> *"Why do you call me 'Lord?' and do not do what I say?"*—LUKE 6:46

The contradictions between what we said we believed and what we were doing with our lives continued to grow. The result was more guilt and shame, more fear, anger, and resentment.

We were saying, "Jesus is Lord," but were unable to do what he asked of us, and what we were promising to do with our lives: serve God, be alert, live soberly, and love one another.

We were living contradictions, destroying ourselves.

But now things are changing.

Now we are becoming more able to call Jesus Lord and do what he asks of us a little bit better. One step at a time. One day at a time.

Working our program.

We aren't perfect, but we are making progress; for which we can give thanks to God.

Am I doing the will of the Lord? Am I doing what I say I believe?

God grant that I may live what I say.

Doing the truth is sobriety.

September 23

BEING CHILDISH

> *"To what, then, can I compare the people of this generation? What are they like?"*—LUKE 7:31

"They are like children sitting in the marketplace and calling out to each other: 'We played the flute for you, and you did not dance, we sang a dirge and you did not cry" (Luke 7:32).

If we couldn't get someone to do what we wanted, we felt hurt and sorry for ourselves. Cheated and childish.

Then we wondered why we turned people off; particularly those who had to be close to us.

Maybe someone told us that we were acting like spoiled children, and indeed it often seemed that way—because we weren't getting our way, the way we wanted it.

So we pouted—if not externally, then internally—and developed resentments.

Now, hopefully, we are growing up.

Now we are growing out of our childish ways.

Am I growing up? Am I letting go of my childishness?

God grant me growing maturity.

Being childish is being cheated.

GIVING GOD THE GLORY

> *"Return home and tell how much God has done for you."*—LUKE 8:39

The demons were gone.

Miraculously.

Finally he was free to be himself—his real, deeper, Christ-self.

Jesus urged him to share the good news; to share it appropriately. To share it with people to whom it could make a difference; people who knew him as he once was, who could know him anew.

Certainly they would notice a difference.

And he was to tell them what the difference was, how he had been saved, how a miracle did for him what he could not have done for himself.

And so it is with us.

"How did you do it?" they ask.

"God did it," we answer.

"We're so proud of you," they say.

"To God be the glory."

Am I giving God the glory? Am I grateful for what the Lord has done and is doing in my life?

God grant me humility and gratitude.

To us go the blessings—to God goes the glory.

September 25

BEING RAISED UP

> *"Don't be afraid; just believe, and she will be healed."*
> —LUKE 8:50

And in some ways we were dead:
Dead to our feelings.
Dead to our value as human beings.
Dead to integrity and dignity.
Deadened to life itself.
There was hopelessness, sometimes despair—terrifying fear and thoughts of suicide.
Then, one day, came a flicker of light that said, "Don't be afraid. Just believe. You too can be brought back to life and healed."
Then God raised us up.
Then we began to take our first steps into new life, new hope, new joy.
That's the way it was.
And that's how it is now.

Am I accepting the healing power of Christ into my life? Am I being raised up, day by day?

God grant that I may be raised up day by day, to newness of life.

Being raised from the dead is a day by day experience.

BEING WHERE WE BELONG

"Master, it is good for us to be here."—LUKE 9:33

They wanted to stay forever in that place, with that experience. But Jesus took them back into the world to shoulder their responsibilities as his disciples, to do their healing work.

Many of us may know how the disciples felt. For we too have been in sharing experiences that we wished could go on and on.

We can say, "It was good for us to be there," at a meeting, a roundup, a celebration of sobriety.

However, like the disciples, we have to go back into the world of everyday living—because that's where our Lord wants us; that's where spiritual growth takes place.

In this sense we also can go back into the world and say, "It is good for us to be here." Right where we are.

Right where the Lord has put us.

Am I where I belong? Am I doing what I have been given to do?

God grant that I may be where I belong, doing my work with joy.

It is good for us to be here and to be sober.

September 27

FOLLOWING JESUS

"I will follow you wherever you go."—LUKE 9:57

The promise he makes to us is not for riches and fame.

On the contrary, he says, "Foxes have holes and birds of the air have nests, but the Son of Man has no place to lay his head."

Sometimes we get confused. We imagine material gains will be added to our sobriety, as a matter of course.

What we *are* promised is that the fear of economic insecurity will leave us.

This happens when we turn our will and life over to the care of God.

What we are guaranteed is spiritual growth—new life, new hope, new joy.

Gratification comes from willingness: "I will follow you wherever you go."

Am I following Jesus where he leads? Am I satisfied with what I am doing with my life?

God grant that I may follow Jesus wherever he leads me.

Following Jesus is the great adventure of all time.

GOING STRAIGHT AHEAD

"No one who puts his hand to the plow and looks back is fit for service in the kingdom of God."—LUKE 9:62

We cannot establish and keep a healthy sobriety if we look back to the "good old days"—or have feelings of regret.

The farmer of old put his hand to the plow behind the ox or the horse and set his eye on the task of cutting the field, straight ahead.

If he looked back, he lost his course and plowed a crooked path. So it is with us and our sobriety.

We look back only in the sense that we remember where we have come from, for this is something we never must forget: How it was. How bad it really was.

Now we have new ground to plow, new seed to plant, new crops to harvest.

We can't do this by lingering in the past.

Now we are engaged in a lifestyle that invites and urges us to go straight ahead with our program, to grow spiritually in our sobriety.

Am I leaving the past behind? Am I going straight ahead with my program?

God grant that I may go straight ahead with my program.

Living with regret is a needless and unproductive waste.

September 29

PRAYING

> *"The harvest is plentiful, but the workers are few. Ask the Lord of the harvest, therefore, to send out workers into his harvest field."*—LUKE 10:2

Our numbers are growing by leaps and bounds, but there is much work to be done.

Millions still are suffering the plague of addiction, going down the drain. A pitiful loss of human life and of our collective humanity.

However, there is something all of us can do about this: We can ask for help.

We can pray the Lord of the harvest to send more workers into the field.

We can ask the Lord to send us.

Mother Teresa was asked, "What can we do to help you in your work with the sick and dying?"

"First of all, you can pray," she said. She did not ask anyone to go with her back to Calcutta.

Nor did she ask for money.

Mother Teresa knows what all of us must learn: Prayer is the energy that ignites new life, new hope, and new joy.

Am I praying regularly? Am I asking God for help?

God grant me the power of prayer.

Prayer is the answer.

KEEPING IT SIMPLE

"Do not take a purse or bag or sandals."—LUKE 10:4

Jesus sent his disciples on a missionary journey without any visible support system, enhancing their power to keep it simple, to concentrate on a given task.

Keeping it simple is important for our sobriety: Be of one mind, don't be cluttered, avoid distractions.

The idea is not to be devoid of support. For Christ is our support. But rather, to concentrate on our mission:

"Whatever God gives me to do today, I intend to do all of it."

The challenge and excitement: Keep it simple, trust God with your life, give as the Lord provides.

Am I keeping it simple? Am I trusting and giving as the Lord provides?

God grant that I may keep it simple, trusting the Lord.

Travel lightly.

October 1

BELIEVING THE PROMISE

> *"I have given you authority to trample on snakes and scorpions and to overcome the power of the enemy; nothing will harm you."*—LUKE 10:19

Our lives had become unmanageable.

There was no hope for recovery, for restoration.

But we finally did admit defeat, finally did surrender to our powerlessness over alcohol, or whatever was keeping us bound.

Finally we did turn our will and life over to God's care and keeping, did receive a new power, a new life force.

Finally we appropriated the promise: "I have given you authority to overcome the power of the enemy, and nothing will harm you!"

Accepting this promise is the very heart of our faith, the foundation for our program and the power to carry on.

Do I believe the promise of Christ? Am I confident that I am safe in his care and keeping?

God grant that I may believe Christ with my whole heart.

Coming to believe Christ's power is the beginning of new life, new hope, new joy.

SEEING NEW THINGS

> *"Blessed are the eyes that see what you see."*—LUKE 10:23

With sobriety, we begin to see new things in new ways.

We see what it means to be brought back to life, not by our own willpower and strength, but by God's grace.

We see how the new life in Christ is available to us, that we need not be in a hopeless condition.

We see our condition as it is, that we are not cured of our addictions, that our spiritual program must be maintained to sustain a healthy sobriety.

We see miracles in our life and the lives of others, where miracles once seemed impossible.

We see how the Holy Spirit moves: quietly, mysteriously, and potently, to bring healing.

We see what it means to be blessed as our gratitude grows.

Am I seeing new things in my recovery? Am I giving thanks to God for them.

God grant me grace to see and celebrate goodness and mercy.

Seeing is believing is living is rejoicing.

October 3

CHOOSING THE BETTER PART

> *"You are worried and upset about many things, but only one thing is needed."*—LUKE 10:41

Remember the anxieties? The fears?

They are not gone, but they are slowly and surely going away as we work our program; because we are choosing a better way of life, learning, and growing.

There still is anxiety.

We still may become upset about many things. But not so much as before.

Slowly but surely, we are choosing new ways to look at life and live it.

Slowly but surely, we are learning to live one day at a time.

Slowly but surely, we are becoming more honest with ourselves, with others, with God.

Slowly but surely, we are learning that only one thing is needed, staying close to Christ.

Slowly but surely, we are carrying this rebirth of the spirit into our activities, maintaining our spiritual base, with our trust in God.

Am I choosing the very best for myself? Am I trusting Christ to lead me?

God grant that I may always have what is needed.

What is needed is what God gives.

TRUSTING THE GOODNESS OF GOD

> *"Which of you fathers, if your son asks for a fish, will give him a snake instead?"*—LUKE 11:11

There were times when it may have seemed as though we were getting the raw end of life's deal, getting dealt a bad hand all the way around.

Even in recovery.

The more we changed, the worse things seemed to get—for a time at least.

It was as though God had it in for us; as though we had asked for something good to happen, but ended up in the midst of a bad joke.

But we came to see and believe that God doesn't specialize in bad jokes, because God is good.

As our recovery progressed, we came to trust the goodness of God in the midst of very difficult times.

After all, we had a lot of unraveling to do, amends to make, and new attitudes to develop. None of which is without pain.

Am I trusting the goodness of God? Am I doing so every day?

God grant that I may live with confidence and trust in goodness and mercy.

God is worthy of our trust.

October 5

UNDERSTANDING ADDICTION

> *"When an evil spirit comes out of a man, it goes through arid places seeking rest and does not find it. Then it says, "I will return to the house I left."'*
> —LUKE 11:24

We must make no mistake about this.

There is no end to addiction, only an end to its practice.

While it may seem that all is done and over, because we do not sense the craving any longer, the addiction, with all of its reaction formations, is prowling, lurking, ready to exert itself again.

"Cunning, baffling, and powerful" describes alcohol and other drugs. They are always ready and eager to return, after being sent away.

Like the evil spirit that says, "I will return to the house that I left."

Today we are sober. And right now that's all that really counts.

Am I overconfident about myself? Do I understand the power of my addiction?

God grant that I may not be complacent about my sobriety.

Overconfidence is the first step away from sobriety.

FILLING EMPTY PLACES

> *"When it arrives, it finds the house swept clean and put in order. Then it goes and takes seven other spirits more wicked than itself, and they go in and live there. And the final condition of that man is worse than the first."*—LUKE 11:25–26

We have removed a huge part of our life and daily living experiences. Something has to replace what once was there.

With abstinence comes vacancies in our lives: What to do with the extra time, the time no longer filled with using?

The empty house has to be filled. But with what?

First go to meetings. Lots of meetings. Ninety meetings in ninety days, if possible.

Read the literature relating to our condition, including the scriptures.

Always remember that an empty place waits to be filled, and so it will be.

Am I filling the empty places with new life, new hope, and new joy? Am I taking good care of myself?

God grant that I may be filled with new life, new hope, and new joy.

God waits to fill our emptiness.

October 7

BEING WILLING TO BE LED

"Blessed rather are those who hear the word of God and obey it."—LUKE 11:28

He came from treatment to AA.

His counselor had told him, "You go and be with those people. And even though you're a very smart person, I want you to sit with them, regularly. And I want you to listen to what they have to say, even though you won't understand much of anything they are saying—not right away. It takes time to catch on to understand what they're talking about.

"And do what they say.

"Don't ask why. Just do it.

"Listen to them and do what they say. Eventually you will understand."

And the man did just that: Attended his meetings regularly. Was attentive to what was said. Listened and obeyed. Became established in his sobriety.

To this day he is grateful for his counselor, who told him, "Listen to what they tell you and do what they say."

Am I listening? Am I obedient?

God grant me the gifts of attentiveness, willingness, and obedience.

Where he leads me, I will follow

TRUSTING THE SPIRIT

> *"The Holy Spirit will teach you at that time what you should say."*—LUKE 12:12

What do I do on a twelfth-Step call?
What do I say?
I don't know much.
I feel so inadequate.
I don't know what to say.
I don't know what to do.
The answer comes from an elder in the program: "What are you so concerned about? You aren't the one who will do the work, who will do the talking. God will do the work. God will do the talking, if any talking has to be done. God will teach you what to say and do.

"And remember this: for you there is no success or failure. For there are no bad twelfth-Step calls."

So it's that simple: We have to learn that God is doing the work through us. The Holy Spirit teaches us what we are to do and say. We have to get ourselves out of God's way.

Am I trusting the Holy Spirit to teach me? Am I trusting God to lead me?

God grant the Holy Spirit to teach me.

Lead me, Lord

October 9

WATCHING OUT FOR OURSELVES

"Watch out! Be on your guard."—LUKE 12:15

"If one drink is good, then two must be better."
We know how that one goes.

So we became greedy for the high, for the uplift-
ing experience that made us feel fulfilled and satisfied.

But that isn't the way it worked.

The more we got into it, the deeper the pit, the
darker the road.

Nevertheless, lingering somewhere within is the
temptation to believe the lie that more of the same
old thing might be better, after all.

Therefore, it's important for us to be on our guard.

We may feel anxious and empty, looking for something or someone to fill the empty places.

However, there are no more quick fixes, no easy
ways out of handling everyday problems.

And more of the same old thing will only get us
dead.

Am I feeling dissatisfied and empty? Am I watching
out for myself?

God grant that I may watch out for my sobriety.

Watching out for ourselves is our first responsibility.

Being Spiritually Fulfilled

> *"A man's life does not consist in the abundance of his possessions."*—LUKE 12:15

Except for the Spirit of God, more of everything does not bring fulfillment. Yet we cannot easily shake the idea that an abundance of possessions will change everything for the better.

Certainly there are rewards to being sober.

On the spiritual journey, we learn that life is more than having an abundance of material possessions; that we must grow out of possessiveness in order to maintain our sobriety—because it was possessiveness that was destroying us.

Now we are able to see that "abundance" is to be spiritually where we belong, in a good working relationship with ourselves, with others, and with God.

Now we are able to see that this has little if anything to do with an abundance of material possessions.

Am I being spiritually fulfilled? Am I finding satisfaction in spiritual things?

God grant that I may be spiritually filled and fulfilled.

The greatest of all possessions can be held only by the heart.

October 11

COUNTERING ANXIETY

> *"Consider the ravens: They do not sow or reap, they have no storeroom or barn; yet God feeds them."*
> —LUKE 12:24

Just because we sober up doesn't mean that we are suddenly set free from anxiety.

As a matter of fact, for a time at least, we may experience a lot more fear and trepidation than ever before.

After all, we did set aside our sedatives and pacifiers, didn't we?

After all, we are now facing the real world, aren't we? And that's a scary place.

Anxiety is not something we are going to dispense with all at once.

However, anxiety spasms do lessen as we work with our fear, as our trust and confidence in God builds, as our sobriety deepens.

Our Lord calmly, confidently, and quietly says to us, "Do not be anxious."

And that is where we must and can begin.

Am I trusting God with my life? Am I turning my fears over to the Lord.

God grant me the gifts of faith and trust.

Don't worry, be happy.

WORRYING USELESSLY

> *"Who of you by worrying can add a single hour to his life? Since you cannot do this very little thing, why do you worry about the rest?"*—LUKE 12:25–26

A spiritual master said to his followers, in short and simple terms, "Don't worry, be happy." And today there are some who are able to do just that— not worry and be happy.

We can't add anything to our lives by worrying, but we can take a lot away.

Knowing this to be true, we can face up to the question of why we worry. The answer can be found in Step Three, where we make a decision to turn our will and life over to the care and keeping of God; also in Steps Six and Seven, where we become willing and ask God to take away all defects of character.

Am I willing to have God remove my defects of character? Am I asking God to remove worry from my life?

God grant that I may be free of useless worrying.

Worry is good for absolutely nothing and even less.

October 13

ESTABLISHING PRIORITIES

> *"Seek his kingdom, and these things will be given to you as well."*—LUKE 12:31

The start-up phrase for a lasting sobriety is, "First things first!"

But we tend to forget what should come first.

Recovery into a good sobriety is based on setting healthy priorities: seeking God's rule, God's power, God's love, and God's life.

Sobriety continues to come day by day, one step at a time, one step after the other. Sobriety is an ongoing process. There is no end to the road, and happily so.

Sobriety is seeking first the kingdom of God: *The kingdom of God is God's rule and will being done in our lives.*

And it is for this purpose that we pray, "Your will be done."

We pray for the will of God to be done, as the first and foremost priority for our new life of new hope and new joy.

Am I putting God first in my life? Am I seeking the kingdom of God, praying for it to come in my life?

God grant the kingdom to come in my life.

There is always more goodness, more blessings to be had.

TRUSTING THE GIVER

> *"Do not be afraid, little flock, for your Father has been pleased to give you the kingdom."*—LUKE 12:32

Don't we already see that we are being blessed?

Don't we remember how it was, and what we longed for in those dark nights of the soul?

Then why are we afraid? Is it not because we forget to trust God, the Giver of new life, new hope, new joy?

We are told by our Lord that God has nothing but the best intentions for us—for our spiritual growth and development.

God is faithful and just. Even when things seem to be going very badly.

We are told, "Do not be afraid."

We are told, "Trust God with your life."

We are told, "It is God's good pleasure to give you the kingdom; God's good pleasure to do what is best for you."

Our job is to trust God.

Our job is to take life in stride.

Our job is to live beyond fear.

Am I trusting God? Am I letting go of my fears?

God grant that I may live beyond fear.

Let God and let go of fear.

October 15

SEEKING TREASURES

"Where your treasure is, there your heart will be also."
—LUKE 12:34

We go after what we really want.

If we don't go after it, we don't want it badly enough.

That's the way things work.

It's important for us to clarify our values to find out who we really are and to strengthen our sobriety.

It's important to decide what we treasure and go for it.

If we are not motivated to gain a treasure, it will not materialize. Sobriety does not materialize and grow until we set our hearts on it.

Until there is dedication to a task, there is no victory.

Working our recovery program helps us point our hearts—our will and desires—in the right direction.

When will and desire are firmed up to do what is best for us, our sobriety is strengthened.

Am I treasuring my sobriety? Am I faithfully working the steps of my program?

God grant that I may treasure my sobriety.

We are what we desire.

BEING DRESSED FOR SERVICE

"Be dressed, ready for service, and keep your lamps burning."—LUKE 12:35

Much of our recovery, a basic part of it, is to be ready for extended service—keeping our lamps burning.

A fundamental purpose of our support groups is to keep the lamps of hope burning, through service.

Service is holding our meetings regularly, so people have a place to gather, share, and support one another.

Service is remaining sober, so people who need it can see God's power at work in us and are given hope.

Service is going to people and places where God leads, offering our experience, hope, and joy.

Being dressed for service is being deeply involved in our program, always ready to be helpful.

Being dressed for service is keeping our lamps of sobriety burning so others can see that change is possible, and give glory to God.

Am I keeping the lamp of my sobriety burning brightly? Am I dressed for service?

God grant that I may keep the lamp of my sobriety burning.

Being sober is being of service to others.

Being Ready and Willing

> *"You also must be ready, because the Son of Man will come at an hour when you do not expect him."*—LUKE 12:40

We never know when or how Christ will come to us in and through another human being in need of help.

Perhaps a phone call at dinner time, or late at night—a call for help.

The strength of our fellowship rests on service in sobriety and very often in the unexpected.

Being "ready" for service means practicing our program, staying close to God through prayer and meditation; attending our meetings regularly; being willing sponsors of those who seek us out.

Being ready and willing is what our program is all about: ready for God to work in our lives; willing to do what is required to stay sober and to serve.

Am I ready and willing to see Christ and serve him in others? Am I ready and willing to do so today?

God grant that I may be ready and willing to serve the Christ in those who come to me.

When we are ready and willing to serve the Christ in others, we are well blessed.

Being Open to All

> *"When you give a banquet, invite the poor, the crip-*
> *pled, the lame, the blind, and you will be blessed.*
> *Although they cannot repay you."*—LUKE 14:13

Nowhere in our fellowship of recovering people is there room for making distinctions as to whom we are willing to serve.

Our fellowship must always be open and inviting. And there is only one qualification for membership: the desire to stop using.

We have no social, economic, political, or educational distinctions; no barriers of race, creed, or religion.

Everyone is invited.

Our program is one of attraction rather than promotion, invitation rather than coercion.

There are no dues.

Nothing is asked of those invited other than the desire to change.

Acceptance and love is extended. Such is the design of our fellowship.

Am I setting any boundaries? Am I open to all who suffer?

God grant that I may be open to all who suffer.

What is not open to all is not open at all.

October 19

BEING FAITHFUL

> *"But they all alike began to make excuses. The first said, 'I have just bought a field, and I must go and see it. Please excuse me.'"*—LUKE 14:18

Procrastination and making excuses, letting important things slip, is something most of us know a great deal about.

Recovery, however, depends on willingness, commitment, faithfulness.

Faithfulness in doing whatever is necessary to grow spiritually.

Faithfulness in following Christ's leading.

Faithfulness in reading our literature, in prayer and meditation.

Faithfulness in attending our meeting, being on hand to support others and to be supported, being ready to serve as a sponsor, carrying the message of recovery.

Am I making excuses? Am I making promises and keeping them?

God grant me to serve, as I have promised.

We have decided to turn our will and our lives over to the care of God.

KEEPING IT SIMPLE

"He who has ears to hear, let him hear."—LUKE 14:35

Important and life-saving things are being said, even when we are in the pits of depression. For instance:

"This too shall pass" (believe it or not).

"It gets better" (even when it feels worse).

"One day at a time" (is the way it works).

"Easy does it" (stop pressing so hard).

"Live and let live" (back off).

"Let go let God (and things will change for the better).

And there's another sentence we say to each other, with love. "Keep it simple . . . stupid."

While others may think we are demeaning ourselves, we know what this means; and how it applies to us.

Am I listening? Am I learning?

God grant that I may listen and learn.

There's nothing so bad that another drink won't make worse.

October 21

UNDERSTANDING OUR PRECIOUSNESS TO GOD

> *"Does he not leave the ninety-nine in the open country
> and go after the one lost sheep until he finds it?"*
> —LUKE 15:4

Knowing that we are important to God is fundamental for our sobriety.

We are precious to God.

And when we are lost, the Lord comes looking for
us.

But we also remember when no one seemed to
care about us, when we didn't care about ourselves,
when we were so physically, emotionally, and spiritually defeated and hopeless.

Then came the day when we had our last drink,
our last fix.

Then came the day when our hearts could sing.

"Amazing grace, how sweet the sound. I once was
lost, but now I'm found!"

Do I believe that God wants me? Do I believe that
I am precious?

*God grant that I may see and believe in my precious-
ness.*

God never stops loving and saving.

MAKING AMENDS

> *"There is rejoicing in the presence of the angels of God over one sinner who repents."*—LUKE 15:10

In Step Four we take an inventory of our character defects, how we have harmed or are harming ourselves and others.

In Step Five we begin to make amends, confessing to God and to another human being "the exact nature of our wrongs," confessing our sins.

In Step Six we are entirely ready to have God remove our defects, our sins.

In Step Seven we humbly ask God to remove our shortcomings, our sins.

In Step Eight we make a list of all people we had harmed and become willing to make amends.

In Step Nine we make direct amends to those we have injured, except when to do so would injure them or others.

In Step Ten we continue to take personal inventory, and when wrong, we promptly admit it.

Am I dealing with my sins and character defects? Am I making amends to myself, to others, to God?

God grant that I am willing to make amends.

Making amends is the key that opens locked doors.

October 23

BEING LOVED BEYOND MEASURE

> *"For this son of mine was dead and is alive again; he was lost and is found."*—LUKE 15:24

The story of the prodigal son cannot be forgotten, not because the prodigal left home and squandered his life in riotous living, but because the loving father waited for him to return.

The father allows his youngest son to work out his own salvation in his own way; even though he ended up eating with the pigs.

And not once did the father say, "I told you so!"

Not once did he threaten, "Don't ever try to come home again!"

Rather, the father prepared a banquet to celebrate the return of his long lost son.

"My son who was lost is found!" he exulted.

This is the way God deals with us; the way God loves, forgives, and welcomes us home—as many times as we choose to return and claim that gift of love.

Am I aware of God's love? Am I grateful for God's love?

God grant that I may always be grateful.

"I have loved you with an everlasting love and you are mine," says the Lord.

BUILDING TRUST

> *"Whoever can be trusted with very little can also be trusted with much, ..."*—LUKE 16:10

Perhaps the greatest loss we suffered while using was the loss of trust.

People simply didn't trust us because we couldn't be trusted—not as we wished we could be.

There were the little lies and deceptions and manipulations that kept us uneasy about ourselves, and kept others uneasy with us.

And when people, especially those close to us, didn't trust us, it hurt our feelings—bringing on self-pity, fear, anger, and resentment.

Now we are learning that honesty is the best policy, that it works for our own betterment, releasing us from binding fear and anxiety.

So we practice honesty in all our affairs, big and little.

Slowly but surely we build trust.

Am I being faithful to my sobriety? Am I building trust?

God grant that I may be honest and faithful in building trust.

Building trust is building a healthy sobriety.

October 25

DOING OUR DUTY

> *"So you also when you have done everything you were told to do, should say, 'We are unworthy servants; we have only done our duty.' "*—LUKE 17:10

Always there is the danger of self-righteous indignation, especially if the progress we believe we are making is not recognized, affirmed—and perhaps praised.

We may be doing everything to stay sober—working the program as best we can, carrying out our duties.

"Isn't it about time for me to get some recognition?" we ask. "A little bit of praise, a pat on the back?"

And what's staying sober worth if people don't affirm us the way we want to be affirmed?

Recovery is enhanced when we are able to rejoice in our sobriety, without having to be reaffirmed or praised by others.

Am I content with myself in my sobriety? Am I expecting honor and glory for staying sober?

God grant that I may be content with myself and my sobriety.

Being true to ourselves is our biggest reward.

BEING HONEST

> *"The Pharisee stood up and prayed about himself;
> 'God, I thank you that I am not like all other men—
> robbers, evildoers, adulterers—or even like this tax
> collector.'"*—LUKE 18:11

Some of us, perhaps many or most, had doubts about the nature or existence of our disease.

After all, we could look around and find people worse off than ourselves—like falling-down drunks, criminals.

We may have come away from meetings saying the very same thing as the Pharisee in Jesus' story—seeing ourselves in a much better condition than others, but missing ourselves completely.

Not to understand and accept this reality is to be deluded.

The truth is that we still are one drink away from a drunk, and one drunk away from being devastated.

Being honest about this is essential to our sobriety.

Am I being self-righteous? Am I seeing myself as being superior to others?

God grant that I may be honest with myself, and about myself.

Being honest about ourselves is staying sober.

October 27

GIVING GLORY TO GOD

> *"Everyone who exalts himself will be humbled, and he who humbles himself will be exalted."*—LUKE 18:14

When it comes to our sobriety, we must forever be on our guard against the conclusion that we have earned it; feeling that we deserve it, that we have rewards coming because we have done such a marvelous work.

Self-exaltation is negative energy, and is always degenerative.

True humility, on the other hand, is positive energy. It makes the best possible use of God's gifts.

Self-exaltation says, "See what I am doing."

True humility says, "See what God is doing."

The emphasis always must be on God—on what God has done and continues to do in and through us:

Paul put it this way: "It is not I, but Christ who lives in me."

Giving glory to God in all that we say and do is the strength of our program. It keeps us humble.

And best of all, it keeps us sober.

Am I humble? Am I giving glory to God?

God grant that I may give glory where glory belongs.

Self-exaltation and staying sober do not go together.

WANTING TO SEE

"Lord, I want to see."—LUKE 18:41

We began to say, if ever so tentatively and softly at first, "I am blind. I want to see!"

But this didn't come easily, because we were afraid of what was inside ourselves: fear, anger, shame, guilt, resentment, and a whole lot more.

The blind man came to Jesus knowing precisely what he wanted for himself.

He asked for what he wanted, and the Lord restored his sight.

And this is our first step into sobriety: wanting to see; becoming willing to look at ourselves the way we really are, with acceptance and surrender.

Trusting in God's will and God's power to see us through.

Believing that seeing is better than not seeing.

Believing that being sober is better than being blind to ourselves.

Am I wanting to see what is real? Am I asking God to help me see?

God grant me the gift of insight, the willingness to look and see who and what I really am.

Reality is easier to deal with than make-believe.

RECEIVING OUR SIGHT

> *"Receive your sight; your faith has healed you."*
> —LUKE 18:42

We began to have faith in God's capacity to restore us to health, and restoration commenced—if ever so faintly.

We asked to see, and light began to infiltrate our souls. Slowly but surely.

We asked for spiritual insight and growth, and our request was granted, although sometimes in painful ways.

We started to sense the restoration of our lives, and in faith continued the pathway of recovery upon which the Lord had placed our feet.

And now it is working for us, this program of recovery:

One day at a time we believe that God has power to heal.

One day at a time we receive our spiritual sight by believing God and working our program.

Am I a believer? Am I beginning to see how it works?

God grant me the infiltration of light, and faith to receive it.

It is not a blast of light that enlightens, but small illuminations.

PRAISING GOD

> *The whole crowd of disciples began joyfully to praise*
> *God in loud voices for all the miracles they had seen.*
> —LUKE 19:37

Sometimes we gather in small groups of two, three, or more, to share what the Lord has done in our lives.

Sometimes we gather in larger groups, even by the thousands, to praise God for redemption.

Praising God.

Giving God the glory. And sometimes with loud voices and whistles do we praise God.

Why?

Because of the miracles experienced in our own lives and the lives of others.

Miracles of rebirth piled up awesomely—one on top of the other.

Skyscrapers of miracles.

Boundless and abounding miracles.

Am I praising God with my life? Am I giving all glory to God?

God grant me a heart filled with praise.

Praising God gives new life to tired souls.

October 31

BLESSING THE NAME OF THE LORD

> *"If they keep quiet, the stones will cry out."*—LUKE 19:40

God's redemption is written into the core of the creation, and the news of salvation cannot be silenced.

But the song was coming from a deeper place; from the very heart of creation itself.

And so it is with us who are experiencing the salvation of our Lord.

Deep inside is the energy of praise, blessing the name of the Lord.

Deep inside is gratitude to God because we recognize the Source of our salvation.

Deep inside we recognize and affirm that God is able to do what no other power can do:

Reach us.

Lift us.

Save us.

Am I aware of God's blessings in my life? Am I praising the name of the Lord?

God grant me a grateful heart.

"Blessed be the name of the Lord!"

GIVING—GIVING—GIVING

"This poor widow has put in more than all the others."
—LUKE 21:3

One thing we begin to learn a great deal about is the value of people, not because of what they have, but because of their capacity to give from the heart—like the widow who gave all she had, while others were giving only a portion of their abundance.

Most invigorating, encouraging, and heartwarming is the abundant giving one experiences in the fellowship of recovering persons, who are faithfully working their program.

The more we give, the more we receive, just as the promises say: "Self-seeking will slip away. Our whole attitude toward life will change. We will lose interest in selfish things and gain interest in our fellows."

As we give, holding nothing back, we find ourselves blessed beyond measure.

Even if we and God are the only ones who know.

Am I a giving person? Am I sharing what has been given me?

God grant that I may give without holding back.

Give, give, give—the threefold way to sobriety.

November 2

PASSING IT ON

> *"I confer on you a kingdom, just as my Father conferred one on me."*—LUKE 22:29

In our recovering fellowship we are blessed with three legacies that have come down through the years—unity, recovery, and service.

In a sense, this is our kingdom, even the kingdom of Christ our Lord.

Christ's singular purpose is to restore the unity of all creation, bringing us back into oneness with ourselves, with others, with God, and the universe.

With unity there is strength and harmony—everything working together for good.

In our fellowship we experience unity as we have not known it before.

Christ also offers recovery, rebirth, and everlasting life.

In our recovery program we begin to experience these gifts: recovering our lives, being reborn into new life, new hope, and new joy.

Am I passing it on? Am I giving to others what is being given to me?

God grant that I may pass on the gifts given to me.

Sobriety is passing it on.

GETTING UP AND PRAYING

> *"Why are you sleeping? Get up and pray so you will not fall into temptation."*—LUKE 22:46

None of us is above and beyond the temptation to use again.

Nor are we able to keep our sobriety on our own, or by force of will.

This is why we are urged to open and close each day with prayer.

Getting up and praying is a very important part of our keeping sober.

There is no power greater than prayer.

And there is no temptation that can withstand the divine energy, the direction, the holiness of prayer.

Self-pity, dishonesty, and self-seeking are three primary temptations we must always guard against with prayer.

We ask God to direct our thinking, especially asking that we be freed from self-pity, dishonesty, and self-seeking.

Complacency is one of our most deadly enemies, and its one certain antidote is prayer.

Am I trusting the power of prayer? Am I praying regularly?

God grant that I may be faithful in prayer.

Prayer is the soul's sincere desire.

November 4

COMING TO REST IN GOD

> *"Father, into your hands I commit my spirit."*—LUKE
> 23:46

Yes, there are times when things come to an end,
sometimes painfully, as they did for Christ our Lord.

Yes, there is suffering, in spite of all we have done
to take care of ourselves.

Yes, we have never been promised a rose garden,
but we have and are always being offered the privilege of coming to rest in God.

"Into your hands I commit my spirit," should be
our constant prayer.

Giving over.

Surrendering.

Offering ourselves up.

Coming to rest in God.

That is the path we are seeking to travel.

That is the way of our Lord, the way to new life,
new hope, and new joy.

Am I committing myself to God? Am I coming to
rest in God?

God grant me a surrendered spirit.

God always is ready to receive and bless our troubled
spirits.

BEING TROUBLED

> *"Why are you troubled, and why do doubts rise in your minds?"*—LUKE 24:38

The last time his disciples had seen their Lord, he was gruesomely dead—and buried.

And should not doubts have arisen in their minds about what they had done with their lives, in relation to him?

After all, they were human.

After all, they had seen him dead and buried.

Hadn't they been given more to bear than could be expected of ordinary people?

After all, they had lost contact with their Lord and were deeply troubled.

So it is with us when we lose contact.

So, day by day, we must be reconnected to ourselves, to others, and to God—through prayer, meditation, and service.

Then no longer are we filled with doubt.

And no longer are our souls troubled.

Am I reconnecting with God each day? Am I turning my troubles and doubts over to the Lord, one day at a time?

God grant me a faithful and trusting heart.

Being connected is the key to an untroubled spirit.

November 6

SEEING AND BELIEVING

> *"Look at my hands and feet. It is I myself! Touch me and see; a ghost does not have flesh and bones, as you see I have."*—LUKE 24:39

Through loving acts of sharing and service, we are touching the Christ in each other.

By presenting ourselves as living testimonies to the power of God, we discover the power of love, the depths of relationship; discover for sure that we are not dealing with illusions or ghosts.

As Christ said to his disciples, "Look at me," we too offer ourselves as living testimonies to the resurrecting power of God at work in the world.

We too may look like ghosts, but we aren't!

"Look at us! See what God has done! We are real people who have come through some very dark valleys. Once we were dead but now we are alive. Touch us, and we will touch you with gifts of new life, new hope, and new joy."

Am I receiving the testimony of God's healing love and power? Am I offering myself as a testimony to God's healing love and power?

God grant that I may see and believe.

Seeing is believing.

BEING AT PEACE

> *"Peace be with you."*—LUKE 24:36

As we progress in our recovery, we realize that peace doesn't just fall out of the sky.

Peace has to be developed through conscious participation on our parts; mainly through prayer and meditation, and trusting God with our lives. Peace is Christ's desire for us: "Peace I leave with you, my peace I give unto you. Let not your hearts be troubled. You believe in God, believe also in me."

It is up to us to keep our hearts free from being troubled, to believe God, to trust our Lord.

We find peace by practicing the presence of Christ; by affirming Christ's presence in the world, at work in our lives.

We find this peace by remembering Christ's promise, "I am with you always."

Christ's desire for us is peace, through confidence in his eternal presence.

Am I practicing the presence of Christ? Am I finding the peace of God in my life?

God grant me abiding peace.

Peace is affirming the presence of Christ in our lives.

November 8

AFFIRMING AND LIVING CHRIST

In the beginning was the Word, and the Word was with God, and the Word was God. He was with God in the beginning.—JOHN 1:1–2

We are tied into the Eternal, to the very beginning of beginnings, tied into God. United, in Christ, with God.

Being aware of what we are working with, and where we are coming from, is stimulating for a growing spiritual life.

From the beginning of creation we have been children of God.

The imprint of the eternal Christ is in each of us—the image of God.

Let us affirm Christ.

Christ—of God.

Christ—from the beginning.

Christ—God to us.

Christ—in us.

Christ—new life, new hope, new joy.

Christ—without end.

Amen.

Am I affirming Christ? Am I living Christ?

God grant that I may affirm and live Christ.

"Just as you received Christ, continue to live in Him."

CELEBRATING TOGETHER

> *Through him all things were made; without him nothing was made that has been made.*—JOHN 1:3

Christ—the blessing of God's grace given to us.

In and through Christ the power of creation is at our disposal, for "through him all things were made".

This is how we come to understand God—through Christ, without whom nothing was made that has been made.

Does this mean that we avoid those who don't have the same vision and affirmation of God as we? No.

Neither does it mean that we compromise our faith in any way. Rather, we quietly join with others who, like ourselves, are working at their recovery in ways that are suitable for them. We celebrate our spiritual growth, in sobriety, together.

Together we are part of all things that are made, as we allow God to do the leading.

Am I celebrating Christ? Am I growing in Christ?

God grant that I may celebrate and grow in Christ.

All of us are united with God, growing in Christ.

November 10

ENJOYING NEW LIGHT AND NEW LIFE

In him was life, and that life was the light of men.
—JOHN 1:4

There was a time when it felt as though we were finding light and life in the bottle, in the drugs.

We didn't find what we were looking for. Our opiates left us miserably defeated and depressed.

At the same time, the gifts of light and life in Christ were waiting for us to admit that we were powerless, waiting for us to believe God—to make a decision to turn our wills and lives over to God's care and keeping.

We began to see the light and life of a new creation.

And best of all, we began to see ourselves as intimate parts of that new creation.

Am I enjoying the new light? Am I enjoying new life?

God grant that I may be filled with new light and new life—and joy.

Light and life—two precious gifts of sobriety to be enjoyed.

WALKING IN THE LIGHT OF A NEW DAY

The light shines in the darkness, but the darkness has not understood it.—JOHN 1:5

We didn't see or understand the light.

Make no mistake about that.

Oh, we may have said words—the words of others. We pretended that we were seeing the light, while going right back into the old life of darkness.

But now we are beginning to see and understand the light that once seemed so far removed.

Now we are beginning to see that it is possible to come into conscious contact with God—slow as that process may be for most of us.

Now the darkness in which we lived is being infiltrated by God's eternal light.

Now, we are able to see the light in others; see the light of God on their faces, see God's light in their expressed hope and acts of love.

Now we see that the darkness is breaking.

Now we see that light is dawning.

Now we are coming home to God, to where we belong.

Am I coming out of darkness? Am I walking in the light of a new day?

God grant that I may walk in the light of a new day.

Light can penetrate the deepest darkness.

November 12

SEEING MORE, DAY BY DAY

The Word became flesh and lived for a while among us. We have seen his glory, the glory of the one and only Son, who came from the Father, full of grace and truth.—JOHN 1:14

Christ came to be with us, especially in all of our pain and confusion.

Through him, God has reached out to us in the flesh, as he reached Mary Magdalene and other destitutes.

Now, the glory of God is seen in the redemption of souls, of people for whom there was no hope.

Now in one another, by faith, the same Christ who lived a human life on earth lives among us and in us.

Now we are in him and he is in us.

Now we are beginning to see his "glory, grace, and truth."

Before the light dawned, we couldn't see.

Now we are beginning to see.

Little by little.

Day by day.

Am I beginning to see glory, grace, and truth? Am I seeing more of Christ, day by day?

God grant that I may see more of Christ, day by day.

Once again—the dawn of a new day.

COMING AND SEEING

"Come, and you will see."—JOHN 1:39

The disciples wanted to know more about Jesus, who he was, where he came from, where he lived.

Jesus worked with their curiosity, which is a primary spiritual energy source.

Jesus invited them, as he invites each of us, to come and see.

Throughout their brief time with Jesus the disciples were given new pictures of him to see, to reflect on, to contemplate.

And they found him in unexpected places: in the homeless, in the hungry, in the sick, in the dying, and in each other.

We too are invited to come and see, and learn more of him.

Am I seeing where Christ lives? Am I offering my service to those who still suffer?

God grant that I may see where Christ lives, and serve him there.

With eyes wide open to the mercies of God, we come to know Jesus.

Being Known and Wanted

> *"I saw you while you were still under the fig tree before Philip called you."*—JOHN 1:48

The secret of the gospel of recovery is that we are known by the Lord before we know him; that we are being watched, and waited for by Christ.

Whether we are drunk or sober, Christ continues to call us.

"Under the fig tree," in certain Eastern idioms, also means "before you were born."

Jesus could have been saying to Nathanael: "I knew you before you were born."

And, to each one of us: "I knew you before you were born. I have been waiting for you to come to me."

Like Philip and Nathanael, we are known and wanted by God.

Am I responding to Christ's call? Am I following Christ?

God grant that I may respond to the call of Christ and follow him.

Answering Christ's call is the beginning of new life, new hope, new joy.

BEING BORN AGAIN

> *"I tell you the truth, unless a man is born again, he cannot see the kingdom of God."*—JOHN 3:3

We know what it is to be born again, because that's what our recovery is about.

Looking back, we say, "And that was my last drink, April 17, 1977, 2:00 A.M. That's when I was reborn!"

One moment we were dead in our addiction, completely unable to stop using.

Then, suddenly and unexpectedly, we stopped.

And with our rebirth, God's light began to glow in the darkness that once filled our souls.

With our rebirth we entered God's kingdom, if only barely.

With God's help we began to work our program, one step at a time, one day at a time, one rebirth after another.

God in Christ—giving us a new birth, one day at a time, as long as we are "entirely willing" to be reborn.

Am I willing to be born again—day by day? Am I coming into newness of life?

God grant that I may be born again, day by day.

Sobriety is spiritual rebirth, one day at a time.

November 16

BEING FREE IN SPIRIT

> *"Flesh gives birth to flesh, but the Spirit gives birth to spirit."*—JOHN 3:6

The "flesh" is the ego—selfish, self-centered, deadly.

The Spirit is life-giving—helping us to rise above ego demands; helping us to live beyond self-destructive desires and attachments.

Self-centered demands give birth to more self-centeredness, more destructiveness.

God-centered desires give birth to new life, new hope, new joy.

When driven by the force of the old self-centered will, we self-destruct.

When led by the Spirit of God, we grow and flourish in our true humanity—the humanity of Christ.

Where once we were self-destructing, we now are coming back to life and growing spiritually.

Am I living in the Spirit? Am I choosing freedom?

God grant that I may live in the Spirit, choosing freedom.

To be free of the old fearful self is to be free indeed.

REMEMBERING

> *"The wind blows wherever it pleases. You hear its*
> *sound, but cannot tell where it comes from and where*
> *it is going. So it is with everyone born of the Spirit."*
> —JOHN 3:8

One night two men carried him into a meeting,
where he slouched in a chair in the back of the
smoke-filled room, too drunk to stand.

They gave him coffee and donuts while a speaker
spoke words he could hardly hear, much less comprehend.

And he never had the need to drink again.

One day we stopped hurting and killing ourselves,
just when it seemed impossible to ever stop using.

And, right then, we didn't know where the power
came from.

But today we know where the power comes from.

The power for us to stay stopped comes from God.

Am I remembering when I couldn't stop? Am I
remembering where the power comes from?

God grant that I may remember the Spirit's power.

There are some things we must remember, and dare
never forget, regardless of how uncomfortable they
may be.

November 18

SPEAKING THE TRUTH

"I tell you the truth, we speak of what we know, and we testify to what we have seen."—JOHN 3:11

We come from a long line of experience, personal and direct.

We come from people who have been there before us, people who knew and know the power of God's power to deliver from bondage.

There is no good reason to doubt their testimony, for none is trying to manipulate or exploit us for selfish purposes.

They simply tell us how it was with them. How God works miracles; how they became conscious of God's power, and how grateful they are for the gift of sobriety.

We too can say, "I tell you the truth. I speak the truth. I tell you of what I have heard and seen."

Am I sharing what I know to be true? Am I telling how it really was, how it really is?

God grant that I may speak the truth of what I have seen and heard.

Sharing what we have experienced is keeping ourselves straight.

Believing and Opening

> *"For God so loved the world that he gave his one and only Son, that whoever believes in him shall not perish but have eternal life."*—JOHN 3:16

"God so loved the world" is the best-known scripture in all of Christendom—spelling out, in one verse, our life and destiny; as we live and abide in Christ.

"God so loved the world" is the most vital of all truths, offering us hope and life, where once there was despair and death.

"God so loved the world" is the good news that undergirds a lasting and growing sobriety.

"That he gave his only Son" is the truth that has changed the lives of millions, all over the world; and continues to do so.

Such is the good news that knows no boundaries, no limitations: "that whoever believes in him shall not perish but have eternal life."

Such is the gift of new life, new hope, and new joy, to all who believe.

Am I believing the promises of God? Am I opening my heart to Christ?

God grant that I may believe and receive Christ as Lord.

The doorway to the Eternal is always open.

Being Saved

> *"For God did not send his Son into the world to condemn the world, but to save the world through him."*—John 3:17

We know that, in and of ourselves, there was no light.

We also know what it is to be rescued from the pits, brought out and stood on our feet.

We know God's purpose for us and the whole world: to save us from ourselves, from sin and death.

And that purpose applies directly to each one of us.

We are not here to be condemned, but to be lifted up and saved from self-destruction.

Regardless of our past.

No matter what we have done to hurt ourselves and others.

We are not here to carry needless guilt and shame.

Rather, our purpose is to serve God with joy and thanksgiving, with an open heart and a free spirit.

Am I living free of condemnation? Am I living my life as a saved human being?

God grant that I may live my life as a saved human being.

Being saved is being free.

LIVING IN THE LIGHT OF TRUTH

> *"But whoever lives by the truth comes into the light,
> so that it may be seen plainly that what he has done
> has been done through God."*—JOHN 3:21

Our program is simple, not simplistic.

We simply attempt to live the truth as it is revealed, day by day.

What stands out in our experience is the presence of truth: truth about ourselves, others, and God.

As we walk in the newness of life, we see more and more of God's reality at work in the world.

We come to understand and believe that whatever good has come our way, beginning with our sobriety, has come through God—God who does for us what we are unable to do for ourselves.

As we practice our program of sobriety, step by step, spiritual awakenings come—sometimes slowly, sometimes quickly.

Each day, as we are open to God's light, there are new infillings of the Spirit, new clarifications of truth, new options for living a sober life.

And all of this is God's doing.

Am I allowing myself to be led by God? Am I coming into new light, day by day?

God grant that I may walk in the light.

We ask God to direct our thinking.

November 22

DRINKING THE LIVING WATER

"Whoever drinks the water I give . . . will never thirst."
—(JOHN 4:14)

When we were thirsty, we certainly didn't think too much about drinking water, except, perhaps as a very small part of a mix.

And whatever our drug of choice, it didn't spring up within us as eternal life, but rather, as certain death.

Christ offers an alternative to such madness: "Whoever drinks the water I give will never thirst."

He is speaking about spiritual gifts such as faith, hope, love, joy, peace, patience, understanding, acceptance, forgiveness, wisdom, and other such blessings.

He is speaking of eternity.

When we allow Christ to be active in our lives, there wells up within us a new spirit: new life, new hope, new joy.

Am I staying close to Christ? Am I drinking the living water of the Spirit?

God grant me the gift of eternal life in Christ.

"Indeed, the water I give . . . will become . . . a spring of water welling up to eternal life." (John 4:14)

WORSHIPING GOD IN SPIRIT AND TRUTH

> *"A time is coming and has now come when the true worshipers will worship the Father in spirit and truth, for they are the kind of worshipers the Father seeks. God is spirit, and his worshipers must worship in spirit and in truth."*—JOHN 4:23–24

Worshiping God in spirit and truth is seeking God through prayer, meditation, and obedience in service—obedience to love.

Worshiping God in spirit and truth is doing for ourselves what is best for us.

Taking good care of our minds, bodies, and spirits.

There are as many forms of worship as there are people.

We choose to worship God together, in various ways because worshiping God in spirit and truth uplifts and gives life.

True worship strengthens our sobriety, providing a way of life that heals and helps.

Am I growing spiritually? Am I worshiping God in spirit and truth?

God grant that I may worship in spirit and truth.

Worshiping God in spirit and truth is giving back what has been given.

November 24

SEEING AND USING WHAT IS OFFERED

"I have food to eat that you know nothing about."
—JOHN 4:32

Spiritual awakening is like going to a great banquet table on which a boundless amount of food awaits us, but we are able to see only a spoon, or a fork, or a roll.

As we take our spoon in hand, there appears a bowl of soup; with the fork comes a potato, with the roll comes some butter. And so it goes as our vision expands—as we begin to see and to know the gifts of God.

What Christ has to offer is inexhaustible, a world without end.

Something new is always being offered.

As Jesus says: "I have food to eat that you know nothing about." And each day, as we are open and ready to receive them, more gifts are given.

Am I seeing what is offered? Am I making use of what is given?

God grant that I may see what is offered and use what is given.

Again, this day, new life is born.

WANTING TO GET WELL

"Do you want to get well?"—JOHN 5:6

The earnest and expressed desire to get well is essential for a growing and lasting sobriety.

"Do you want to get well?" Jesus asks us.

For us, the answer is "yes."

Yes, we do want to get well, or we wouldn't be doing what we are doing—trying to stay sober.

But sometimes, perhaps we say yes with tongue in cheek, with compliance rather than surrender: "Yes, I want to get well. But, I also want feel sorry for myself. And resentful. Because I can't use anymore."

So the question persists: "Do you *really* want to get well?"

And if not—then what?

Do I really want to get well? Am I asking God for help?

God grant that I may always have a desire to heal.

Wanting to get well is the first step to getting well.

November 26

ASSUMING RESPONSIBILITY FOR OUR LIVES

"See, you are well again. Stop sinning or something worse may happen to you."—JOHN 5:14

There was a healing pool, but the paralytic never got to the healing waters in time.

Maybe he stationed himself too far away from the pool on purpose, keeping himself in a position where it was not possible for him to get healed.

Perhaps he was malingering, procrastinating, refusing to take responsibility for his life and well-being—deciding to stay stuck in one place.

And maybe his sin was just that: deciding to stay stuck and helpless.

We know something about this destructive attitude.

We have had our own stint with denial, malingering, procrastination, the refusal to take responsibility for our attitudes and behavior.

But we now know where the healing waters are and how to stay close to them.

Am I taking responsibility for my life? Am I doing what is necessary to heal and to grow?

God grant that I may take responsibility for my life, to heal and to grow.

If not I—then who?

Doing What We See Being Done

> *"I tell you the truth, the Son can do nothing by himself; he can do only what he sees his Father doing, because whatever the Father does the Son also does."*
> —JOHN 5:19

Jesus designed his life in a particular way, in relationship to God—which also is a good design for our staying sober.

He accepted responsibility for his life and mission, but did nothing without being led by God.

What he saw God doing, he did.

In our first three recovery steps we attempt the same attitude and way of life.

We turn to God to direct the course of our lives.

We look to the mercy and love of God as a way of life that we want for ourselves.

What we see Jesus doing, we seek to do; as our commitment and gratitude to him deepens.

Am I seeing what Jesus does? Am I doing what Jesus does?

God grant that I may see and do what Jesus does.

We are doing what we see being done—and we are recovering.

November 28

BEING RAISED UP

> *"For just as the Father raises the dead and gives them life, even so the Son gives life to whom he is pleased to give it."*—JOHN 5:20

We must make no mistake about this: we are recipients of God's gifts.

We are being raised from the dead and given new life—as gifts from God.

There is nothing of this goodness and mercy that we have earned or deserved; nothing that can be bought or sold.

However, we can share what has been given, and others can share with us.

It is in the sharing of God's gifts that new life, hope, and joy are added to us.

As Christ is pleased to give to us, we are asked to give to others.

In so doing we see death turned into life—slowly but surely.

Am I willing to be spiritually raised up day by day? Am I willing to experience new life, new hope, and new joy?

God grant that I may be raised up to newness of life.

"Praise to the Lord, for he showed his wonderful love to me." (Psalm 31:21)

CROSSING OVER

> *"I tell you the truth, whoever hears my word and be-*
> *lieves him who sent me has eternal life and will not*
> *be condemned; he has crossed over from death to life."*
> —JOHN 5:24

When we become sober, we begin the crossover from death to life.

No doubt about that.

Things begin to become that different for us: from death to life.

Not that we leave our old self behind altogether, for certainly we don't.

We may bring deep feelings of condemnation, guilt, and shame, but we needn't.

Instead, we can listen to the words of promise: "Whoever hears my word and believes God, has eternal life and will not be condemned."

By believing God's love and forgiveness, we cross over from death to life; beyond guilt, shame, and condemnation.

Am I hearing the promises of Christ? Am I crossing over from death to life?

God grant that I may cross over from death to life.

Sobriety is going from death to life.

November 30

BEING SPIRITUALLY SATISFIED

> *"I am the bread of life. He who comes to me will never go hungry, and he who believes in me will never be thirsty."*—JOHN 6:35

We used excessively to satisfy a deep longing, to fill empty places, to cover fear, to find comfort and peace.

We also had a deep longing for God.

We were hungry for God and didn't really know it.

We were lost souls seeking our source.

Now we know more about our need to be spiritually satisfied.

It is all part of the recovery process:

Having had a spiritual awakening, we are beginning to see new glimmers of God's light.

We are beginning to be spiritually satisfied.

As long as we believe God and continue coming to Christ, our spiritual hunger and thirst will be satisfied.

Am I turning to Christ? Is my spiritual hunger and thirst being satisfied?

God grant that I may be spiritually satisfied.

To live and believe Christ is to be spiritually satisfied.

BELIEVING THE PROMISE

> *"All that the Father gives me will come to me, and whoever comes to me I will never drive away."*—JOHN 6:37

Jesus promises to accept us totally, never to drive us away or cast us aside. And this is very important, especially for those of us who have, by our own faults and behavior, put ourselves in a position to be set aside by others, even cast out.

The good news is that we will not be driven away.

The good news is that we are in the care and keeping of Christ.

We can always go to Christ, always do a fifth Step with him, day by day.

Never having to hide anything.

Always knowing that we are acceptable.

Just the way we are.

Never, ever to be cast aside.

So great is the truth of God. So great is the love of Christ.

Am I believing the promise of Christ? Am I certain that I will never be cast aside?

God grant me a believing, trusting, grateful heart.

God hasn't created us to be thrown away.

December 2

BEING WATCHED OVER

> *"And this is the will of him who sent me, that I shall lose none of all that he has given me."*—JOHN 6:39

The good news is that we are in the care and keeping of the Lord, who is not going to let us get lost.

We have been entrusted into his personal care and keeping.

We are being looked after and cared for.

And this is very comforting; especially when we remember our former condition of being so isolated and separated from ourselves, from others, from God.

The promise is that never will we be lost.

Never will we be separated from the care and keeping of the Good Shepherd.

We are always being looked after.

We are always being cared for.

We are always of value to God.

Am I placing my confidence and hope in Christ? Am I trusting the Lord to watch over me?

God grant that I may place my confidence and hope in Christ, trusting him to watch over me.

Jesus will never let us go.

APPROPRIATING GOD'S GIFTS

> *"My Father's will is that everyone who looks to the Son and believes in him shall have eternal life."*
> —JOHN 6:40

Before becoming sober, we were in bondage, unable to connect, to become part of, to work together.

Now, however, we are able to know and believe God.

Now we are able to know and believe that we are part of God in Christ, and part of one another.

Now we can know and believe that it is God's Son who reveals the truth of God to us.

Now we know and believe that we have eternal life.

Now we are able to appropriate what God offers.

With sobriety we are being set free to believe and to do God's will, to inherit the many gifts of the kingdom—including life eternal.

Am I believing God's offered gifts? Am I appropriating the gifts?

God grant that I may believe and appropriate the gifts of eternal life.

Once we see and accept life as eternal, all else is open to us.

December 4

BEING MADE ALIVE FOREVER

"I am the living bread that came down from heaven. If anyone eats of this bread, he will live forever."
—JOHN 6:51

The promises of the gospel are based on historical experience.

For instance, the experience of the children of Israel in their wilderness wanderings.

Being fed by God with manna from heaven.

Having their thirst quenched by water that came from a rock.

Christ says he is bread, that he is eternal life come down from heaven—that whoever eats of this bread will live forever.

The more we listen to Christ, the more we believe him, the more we follow in his footsteps, and the more we become filled with his spirit—the more apparent it becomes that, in Christ Jesus, we are going to live forever.

We are in the process of being made alive—forever!

Am I being spiritually fed? Am I living forever?

God grant that I may be filled with Christ and be alive forever.

Christ is our lifeline forever!

RECEIVING CHRIST

> *"This bread is my flesh, which I will give for the life of the world."*—JOHN 6:51

Taking upon himself all of our defects, all of our pain and suffering, Christ showed us the way through every difficulty, every barrier, even through death itself.

Christ offered himself as a sacrifice, showing us a way of life that extends beyond the cross, beyond death and dying.

Christ gives himself for the life of the world, and that includes all of us.

Christ invites us to accept what is being offered—invites us to receive him as our Lord and master, as our savior and friend.

Where would we be without Christ?

Am I accepting what is being freely offered? Am I receiving Christ as my Lord and master, savior and friend?

God grant that I may receive Christ as my Lord and master, savior and friend.

Receiving Christ is receiving life that is forever.

December 6

REMEMBERING AND LIVING FOREVER

"Whoever eats my flesh and drinks my blood has eternal life."—JOHN 6:54

Jesus is talking about the closest possible communion, which turns into eternal life.

However, not until we begin to detoxify are we able to get on with our recovery, to sense a real need for a lot more of God's grace.

It is then that we begin to understand that we must get closer to God, and to Christ.

Just as the children of Israel ate God-given manna in the wilderness and were saved, so now Christ is offered as the bread of life, to be spiritually eaten and digested.

As we commune together at the Lord's table we are remembering and receiving the gift of eternal life, through him who says, "Do this in remembrance of me."

Am I remembering Christ? Am I receiving Christ into my life?

God grant that I may remember and receive Christ into my life, day by day.

Staying close to Christ is staying alive and well.

FINDING NEW LIFE IN CHRIST

> *"This is the bread that came down from heaven. Our forefathers ate manna and died, but he who feeds on this bread will live forever."*—JOHN 6:58

The starving people in the wilderness ate of the manna and lived a bit longer, but then they died.

Christ, however, is eternal bread.

When we "eat" Christ—ingest him spiritually—we begin to see something new. We begin to see eternal life, world without end.

By tying into Christ, we tie into the Eternal One, who always has been the creative force, the energizing element, the Word of God made flesh and blood, the essence of life itself.

Whoever feeds on Christ feeds on life, and will live forever.

The bottle, the pills—all were temporary. All gave the promise of life, and all failed us miserably.

Christ, on the other hand, is real and alive, and never failing.

Am I feeding spiritually on Christ? Am I finding new life, new hope, and new joy in the Lord?

God grant that I may find new life in Christ, day after day.

Christ is forever.

COMING TO BELIEVE

> *"Yet there are some of you who do not believe."*
> —JOHN 6:64

We do not become staunch believers in God all at once. Not in the sense that Christ believed.

But day by day, we are coming to believe God more and more.

More of God in Christ.

More of God in the world.

More of God in us.

Yes, we still may be virtual unbelievers, with anxiety about this day and the days to come:

Because our memories are short.

Because we are forgetful.

Because we don't always remember the miracles of God in our life.

Because we forget God's miracles in the lives of others.

However, with the passing of each day, as we work our program, one day at a time, we are coming to believe God a little bit more.

As we practice the presence of God through prayer, through meditation, through service.

Am I believing God? Is my faith in Christ growing?

God grant that I may be a true believer.

I believe. Help my unbelief.

COMING FROM GOD

> *"My teaching is not my own. It comes from him who sent me."*—JOHN 7:16

Our program did not come from a single person or even from that first little group. It came from God.

And the teachings we have are not ours alone. They come from another—from God. Teachings of acceptance and forgiveness, of love of sharing and rejoicing in hope.

Ours is a supernatural program for recovery, beyond human invention, outside the realm of self-devised imagination.

Our teachings are not our own. They have come to us from above. And this is what makes it work, because it is timeless, and flawless.

When we work the steps, doing the program, not only do we grow in grace, we flourish.

Because everything is coming from God.

Am I aware that strength and hope comes from God? Am I giving all glory to God?

God grant that I may never forget where all the gifts are coming from.

Every good and perfect gift comes from God.

HONORING GOD

> *"He who speaks on his own does so to gain honor for himself, but he who works for the honor of the one who sent him is a man of truth; there is nothing false about him."*—JOHN 7:18

If we get ourselves in the way, we mess up.

That has been our experience.

We dare not forget it, lest we do it again and get lost once more.

We may tell people about ourselves, how it was, and how it is now. But our real message is about the love and mercies of God.

While it is good to be happy about ourselves— even with a touch of healthy pride—honoring God must be our ministry and life.

Trying to gain honor for ourselves results in uncomfortable feelings.

When, however, we are honoring God, no longer do we feel out of sorts with ourselves.

Because, when we are giving God the glory, we are not speaking on our own, to gain honor for ourselves.

Rather, we are speaking and living the truth.

And, there is nothing false about us.

Am I honoring God? Am I giving all glory to God?

God grant that I may give honor where honor is due.

Honoring God is the heartbeat of sobriety.

BELIEVING IN CHRIST

> *"Whoever believes in me, as the Scripture has said, streams of living water will flow from within him."*
> —JOHN 7:38

Out of the side of a hill it comes, a spring of living water.

And people are there to fill up their jars, jugs, and pails, because the water is abundant and pure—healthy and life-giving.

When we are gratefully sober, we become like that spring and God is able to use us as life-giving resources to others—as givers of new life, new hope, and new joy.

The gifts of sobriety are like life-giving water to parched land. Where once there was lifelessness, new life begins to germinate.

Where once there was no hope, new hope takes root.

Where once there was none, new joy begins to blossom.

Am I placing my faith in Christ? Is new life, hope, and joy flowing from within me?

God grant that I may be like a stream of living water.

Believing in Christ is opening ourselves to new life, new hope, and new joy.

December 12

> *"I am the light of the world. Whoever follows me will never walk in the darkness, but will have the light of life."*—JOHN 8:12

No one has to tell us what it feels like to be in the dark night of the soul.

We wanted light, but could not see.

One day, however, something happened that changed the course of our lives.

Light dawned.

Not a sudden and blinding sunburst, but more like a little flicker of a candle; just enough to make a difference, to catch our attention, to help us say, "This is the first day of my life."

The light of God came upon us, and we began to walk in that light, soberly.

Now we are becoming able to hear Christ's promise: "I am your light. If you follow me, you will never have to walk in that darkness again."

Am I walking in the light of Christ? Am I seeing the dawning of a new day?

God grant that I may walk in the light of a new day.

Walking in the light is the dawning of new days yet to come.

BEING SET FREE

> *"If you hold to my teaching, you are really my disciples. Then you will know the truth, and the truth will set you free."*—JOHN 8:31

As we hold to the experience and teachings of our Lord, we slowly but surely begin knowing what is true—begin tasting a new-found freedom of heart, mind, and spirit.

It's like Jesus said, "If you hold to my teaching, you will know the truth and the truth will set you free."

The teachings we hold to are from Christ, whether they come directly from Holy Writ, or are funneled through other books and pamphlets, and and people.

And, as we become doers of the steps, practicing these principles in all our affairs, we are indeed, following Christ.

We are, indeed, doing the truth that is setting us free.

Am I working the Steps? Am I following Christ, doing the truth, being set free?

God grant that I may know the truth and do it.

Being set free is being sober.

December 14

BEING GLORIFIED

> *"If I glorify myself, my glory means nothing."*—JOHN
> 8:54

Some of us have been glorified through persecution, torture, and martyrdom.

Others have been glorified in the limelights of material success—receiving the adulation of people.

Most of us, however, are glorified in less spectacular means—primarily in quiet and oft unpublicized acts of servanthood.

And as Christ teaches, real glory must come from God, not from other people.

For, apart from God, we can do nothing.

If we glorify ourselves, our glory is in vain.

If we glorify ourselves, others only see the vanity of self-centeredness, rather than the glory of God at work in our lives.

For we are truly glorified—by God alone.

Am I being glorified by God? Am I giving all glory to God?

God grant that I may be set free from all bondage to self.

"I no longer live but Christ lives in me." (Galatians 2:20)

BEGINNING AT THE BEGINNING

> *"I tell you the truth, before Abraham was born, I am!"*
> —JOHN 8:58

The claim of the Christ of God is from all eternity, no beginning, no end.

The statement of power is in two words—"I AM!"

Before Abraham.

Before anyone.

Alpha and Omega, the beginning and the end.

It is this Christ whom we are trusting to help us along the path, to keep us strong, straight, and clean.

Christ in us, the hope of glory!

We aren't dealing with secondary powers, but with the power of creation itself.

Each day we can begin anew with new joy and expectation, knowing that the "I AM" of all creation is here, working in and through us to will and to do.

Am I beginning at the beginning in my recovery? Am I beginning with Christ?

God grant that I may begin and end each day with Christ my Lord.

"The life I live in the body, I live by faith in the Son of God, who loved me and gave himself for me." (Galatians 2:20)

December 16

TRUSTING THE GOOD SHEPHERD

> *"I am the good shepherd. The good shepherd lays down his life for the sheep."*—JOHN 10:11

Slowly but surely, we began to see a new and vibrant power of love at work in our lives.

Slowly but surely, we began to believe God with our hearts and minds.

Slowly but surely, we began to trust the One who laid down his life for us and for our salvation.

Slowly but surely, we began to live and grow spiritually:

Admitting we were powerless, that our lives were unmanageable.

Believing that the power of God could restore us to sanity.

Making a decision to turn our will and our lives over to the Good Shepherd of our souls.

Am I trusting God's power? Am I turning my will and my life over to Christ, the Good Shepherd of my soul?

God grant that I may trust Christ, the Good Shepherd, with my life.

To you, my Lord, I lift up my soul. O Good Shepherd, I trust in you.

BELIEVING LIFE ETERNAL

> *"I am the resurrection and the life. He who believes
> in me will live, even though he dies; and whoever lives
> and believes in me will never die. Do you believe this?"*
> —JOHN 11:25–26

We were scared of living and scared of dying.

As the fog lifted in our brains, we became more
conscious of life and death—became more aware of
time, that we don't have much of it left.

We became more conscious of life rushing by so
rapidly, we felt sad for having wasted so much of it.

The thought of death—our own or that of our
loved ones—could leave us despondent, worried, and
unsure of ourselves.

Sober, however, we are better able to hear and
believe the promise of everlasting life: "As he lives
we also shall live!"

Is there anything about sobriety that is better than
knowing this?

Am I a believer? Do I believe that I have life eternal?

*God grant that I may accept and celebrate the gift of
eternal life.*

Morning is breaking.

December 18

SEEING THE GLORY OF GOD

> *"Did I not tell you that if you believed, you would see the glory of God?"*—JOHN 11:40

We have seen and are seeing the glory of God.

As we move along in our program, we become more aware each day that life is something beyond anything we ever knew.

There's a new sense of glory, of resplendent magnificence, that comes with sobriety.

Not all at once, to be sure.

Most often we see the glory of God only with little glimpses, here and there, now and then.

However, the more we stay in conscious contact with Christ and our program, the more we see the glory of God at work in others, and ourselves.

Am I seeing the glory of God revealed in Christ, in myself, in others? Am I celebrating God's glory with joy and thanksgiving?

God grant that I may see the glory of the Lord in myself and others.

There is no end to the resplendent magnificence of God.

BEING UNBOUND AND SET FREE

"Take off the grave clothes and let him go."—JOHN 11:44

And Lazarus arose.

Then the grave clothes that bound his body, were taken off—as Lazarus was returned to his loved ones, to life and living.

What better analogy is there than to liken ourselves to Lazarus? For were we not dead? Were we not separated from loved ones, locked in our tombs? Bound up? Sealed in? Behind closed doors?

And didn't there have to be a miracle to bring us back?

Didn't we have to become unbound physically, mentally, and spiritually?

And isn't it true that no longer do we have need for grave clothes, the tomb, and locked doors?

Like Lazarus we have been raised from the dead.

Praise be to God!

Am I unbound? Am I set free?

God grant that I may be unbound and set free.

"Break forth, o beauteous heavenly light, and usher in the morning." (Hymn by Johann Schup)

December 20

TRUSTING THE LIGHT

> *"Put your trust in the light while you have it, so that you may become sons of light."*—JOHN 12:36

Where did we place our trust and confidence? Remember?

We placed our trust in the wrong places, things, and people.

Rather than becoming sons and daughters of light, we became sons and daughters of gloom and darkness.

Now, however, we see the light of God at work in hearts and minds.

Now we are looking to God for new life, new hope, and new joy.

By trusting in Christ, the light of the world, we are learning to live as sons and daughters of God.

Slowly but surely, we are finding what we always have been seeking: comfort, peace, and tastes of serenity.

New life, new hope, new joy.

Am I seeing the light of God? Am I living in that light?

God grant that I may learn to live Christ.

To live in the light is to live Christ.

WALKING IN THE LIGHT

"Walk while you have the light."—JOHN 12:35

Now is the time for us to live in the light of God's love. Now we must not hesitate to move on.

When we see light, we must go for it, without compromising, without letting up.

We must be aware that the old character defects are still hanging around—like the tendency to let up on healthy and life-giving pursuits; such as regular reading of our literature, regular attendance at meetings, regular prayer and meditation, and regular acts of service.

When things are going well or badly, the tendency is to slip. That has been our experience.

Not because we are bad people, but because we lose our focus, taking our eyes off the goal of a growing and maturing spiritual rebirth.

While we have the light of Christ, we must walk in it, lest we find ourselves, once again, wandering around in the snake pits of darkness from which we have been so mercifully lifted.

Am I doing first things first? Am I walking in the light?

God grant that I may walk in the light.

Light of light enlighten me. A new day is dawning.

December 22

STAYING IN THE LIGHT

> *"I have come into the world as a light, so that no one who believes in me should stay in darkness."*—JOHN 12:46

There are places we should stay, and there are dangerous places and situations we must avoid.

The old hangouts are to be avoided, simply for self-protection, whether that hangout is the corner bar or a closet.

Also, we must not get too hungry, too tired, too angry, too lonely.

To avoid the darkness, we must stay in the light, doing whatever has to be done to maintain our God-given sobriety.

Christ Jesus provides the light we need to stay clean and sober today.

Believing Christ is trusting him to manifest his light in us.

Following Christ means that we no longer need to stay in the darkness of gloom and doom.

Am I believing and following Christ? Am I staying out of dark places?

God grant that I may stay in the light.

"The light shines in darkness." (John 1:5)

COMING TO UNDERSTAND

> *"You do not realize now what I am doing, but later you will understand."*—JOHN 13:7

We don't understand how God can be so persistent about redeeming us, who otherwise would be lost in darkness and death.

We don't fully understand the sacrifice, Christ's willingness to lay down his life for us, to show us the way to God.

Little by little, we can see and believe that God works in mysterious ways.

One step at a time, we are becoming more able to see and understand that God is mightily at work in the world and in our lives.

Bit by bit, we are coming to understand how it works: " 'Not by might, not by power, but by my Spirit,' says the Lord."

Am I coming to understand? Am I beginning to see how God is working in the world and in my life?

God grant that I may grow in my understanding of how it works.

Understanding the ways of God is a process of human development, one step at a time.

December 24

MINISTERING CHRIST

> *"Unless I wash you, you have no part with me."*
> —JOHN 13:8

Simon Peter balked. "Lord, you shall never wash my feet!"

"Unless I wash you, you have no part with me," Jesus replied.

"Lord, not just my feet only but also my hands and my head!" was Peter's answer.

By this lowly act, Jesus provided the model for his followers, for all time to come: servanthood.

We are called to be servants, helping other people to live. And with this comes renewal—ours and theirs.

To see people recover, to watch them help others, to see loneliness vanish, to see a fellowship grow up about us, to have friends—this is an experience not to be missed.

Am I allowing Christ to minister to me? Am I ministering Christ to others?

God grant that I may serve as I am being served.

"Take my life and let it be, consecrated, Lord, to thee." (Hymn by Wm. Henry Havergal)

SERVING AS SERVANTS

> *"Do you understand what I have done for you?"*
> —JOHN 13:12

Jesus finished washing his disciples' feet and said, "Do you understand what I have done for you?"

Certainly they felt the power of such humility in service, and that feeling would not go away.

That memory would follow them for the rest of their lives.

Their lives had been radically changed.

All of their fear and self-seeking had been addressed in this singular and simple act of servanthood.

The Lord had touched them in a dynamic and unexpected way.

And this act of humble servanthood would help set them free from the bondage of self—once they had time to reflect on what their Lord had done for them.

Am I understanding the power of servanthood? Am I being a servant of Christ to others?

God grant that I may understand and live the power of servanthood.

It works. It really does.

December 26

EXTENDING LOVE

> *"A new command I give you: Love one another."*
> —JOHN 13:34

Love keeps us in fellowship.

Love of God—love for one another.

"Love" an easy word to say in songs—thousands and thousands of them—saying, "I love you." Or "God loves you and so do we!" Or, "Let's make love."

It's popular to say it, to imagine it, to play with the idea.

But actually to love is another matter.

An important spiritual exercise says: "Do something for someone today without their knowing who did it." That's one portrait of love actualized in service.

Love, actualized in service, is the binding glue of human relationships and spiritual growth.

Am I accepting Christ's love into my life? Am I extending the love of Christ to others?

God grant that I may extend the love of Christ to others.

Love is patient and kind. Love is not jealous or boastful. Love does not insist on its own way.

BEING FAITHFUL DISCIPLES OF CHRIST

"All men will know that you are my disciples if you love one another."—JOHN 13:35

While we may have wanted to view ourselves as being very loving persons, the truth is that it was not possible. Not in our condition. Not with our disease of self-centeredness running wild.

Now, however, some of that is beginning to change.

As we live and work our program, the emphasis is on love—giving to others as Christ gives to us; offering a cup of cold water in his name to the thirsty, and bread to the hungry.

Discipleship is framed in love, in servanthood.

It was love that came to us when we were in the darkness of death.

It was love that lifted us.

It is love that is giving us new life, new hope, with new joy.

Am I becoming a faithful disciple of Christ? Am I offering Christ's love to others?

God grant that I may be a faithful disciple of Christ.

What we do for others is done for Christ.

December 28

TRUSTING GOD

> *"Do not let your hearts be troubled. Trust in God; trust also in me."*—JOHN 14:1

Consciously or unconsciously, all of us are concerned about being abandoned.

This fear of being separated from ourselves, others, and God is part of the human condition.

So it was with the disciples of Christ.

They were deeply troubled about the Lord's leaving them.

The feared emptiness was too much for them.

They had to be reassured that everything was going to be all right.

And so do we.

Their hearts were troubled, and understandably so.

And Jesus said something very simple and direct to them: "Don't be troubled. Trust God! Trust me!"

If we are able to get that piece of work done in our recovery—trusting God in Christ—we need never be afraid of being left alone again.

Am I afraid? Am I trusting God?

God grant me a heart filled with trust.

God knows where you are, and God cares.

HAVING A PLACE PREPARED FOR US

> *"In my Father's house are many rooms . . . . I am going there to prepare a place for you."*—JOHN 14:2

The disciples were unsure and afraid, because the Lord was leaving them.

And where he was going, they could not come.

Not right away.

However, one day they would be with him again, in a place prepared for them.

The care of the Lord for his friends, for all of us, is the good news of the gospel.

We are wanted and are being cared for.

In the meantime, we have work to do in the here and now. Especially work on ourselves.

Spiritual work: the work of spiritual growth and development—in faith, hope, and love.

We needn't wonder what is going to happen to us now, or in the world to come.

Because a place is already prepared for us.

Am I confident about the future? Do I believe that there is a place for me?

God grant me gifts of trust, confidence, and gratitude.

There is a place for us.

December 30

RECEIVING THE SPIRIT

> *"I will ask the Father, and he will give you another Counselor to be with you forever—the Spirit of truth."*
> —JOHN 14:16–17

The disciples were not to be left comfortless.

Although Christ would leave them physically, he would come to them, as the Spirit of truth—the Holy Spirit.

By this promise they could be comforted.

Beginning with Pentecost they came to count on the counselor, the Holy Spirit of truth.

For it was the Spirit that energized them and kept the message of the gospel alive in the world.

We too can count on the Holy Spirit to be with us, to work through us.

We too can be in an attitude of trust and confidence in God, because the Spirit never fails us.

The Spirit of truth is the Spirit of Christ at work in ourselves and others.

Am I open to the Holy Spirit? Am I receiving the Spirit's gifts?

God grant that I may be open to the gifts of the Spirit.

"Come Holy Spirit, God and Lord." (Hymn by Erfurt Gesangbuch)

BEING ALIVE IN CHRIST

> *"Because I live, you also will live."*—JOHN 14:19

No matter how far down the scale we have gone, we see how our experience can benefit others.

That feeling of uselessness and self-pity is disappearing. We are losing interest in selfish things and gaining interest in our fellows.

Self-seeking is slipping away.

Our whole attitude and outlook on life is changing.

Fear of people and economic insecurity is leaving us.

We realize that God is doing for us what we cannot do for ourselves.

Are these extravagant promises?

We think not.

They are being fulfilled among us—sometimes quickly, sometimes slowly.

They always materialize if we work for them.

Am I being alive in Christ? Am I living the promises?

God grant that I may be alive in Christ.

Glory to God in the highest, and on earth—peace.